R.L. PELSHAW

ILLEGAL *to* LEGAL
Business Success for (ex)Criminals

R.L. PELSHAW

AVAILABLE FOR PURCHASE AT:

illegaltolegal.org

Truth About Prison – Network (TAP-X) Store:
truthaboutprison.com/store.html

createspace.com/4933768

amazon.com

and fine bookstores

AVAILABLE FOR SPEAKING ENGAGEMENTS THROUGH:

The Pelshaw Group
PO Box 460671
Papillion, NE 68046
402-932-7777
info@illegaltolegal.org

This book is dedicated to
Anyone who ever made money from crime
And wants a fresh start.

My prayer is that God helps you
To find a fulfilling new life,
And that you help someone else
Along the way.

TESTIMONIALS FOR
"ILLEGAL TO LEGAL"

"This book gives the one thing that is almost priceless in prison and that is hope. After reading "Illegal to Legal" you realize that hope can turn into reality if you just don't give up and focus on the skills you have had all along, but never realized."
-J Musso, Founder of TAP-X
Truth About Prison Network

"I wish I knew about this when I was on the street, maybe I wouldn't be here right now."
-"Big O", Inmate

"I absolutely love your book and wish I could put it into the hands of every prisoner who is going to be released; it would sure help prevent their return to incarceration."
-Suzanne Powell, Book´Em
(A Pittsburgh based non-profit providing books to prisoners)

"For the first time since getting locked up I have hope for a good life when I'm free."
-"Big Mo", Inmate

"Of everything I've read in prison this is the best thing yet, and the only thing to really help me be successful on the outside. Every inmate and every ex-offender should read this book."
-"Damon O", Former Inmate

"This book will help a lot of people go from a drug business to a legit business."
-"Ike", Inmate

"This book, and Bob Pelshaw, has helped my life a lot. Lots of people told me "to do the right thing," but Pelshaw showed me exactly how I could succeed doing that."
-"Tango" Thomas Washington, former inmate

TABLE OF CONTENTS

ABOUT THE AUTHOR

Bob Pelshaw was a successful Midwestern real estate broker, developer, and consultant specializing in free-standing retail projects for national and regional retailers, private shopping centers, office buildings, multi-family projects, and leadership development. His twenty-five year career included service as a state officer for the International Council of Shopping Centers (ICSC) plus more than $640 million in career transactions. Along the way he also invested in and consulted for various other types of businesses including laundromats, a janitorial company, a brokerage, convenience stores, grocery stores, retail stores, a car wash, a restaurant, barber shops, construction companies, a resort hotel, property management, rental properties, self-storage facilities, a health club, marketing organizations, and others.

Pelshaw served numerous non-profit groups including being a director and officer for the local Big Brothers Big Sisters Chapter, his church, and most notably as an associate trainer for Dr. John C. Maxwell's global non-profit ministry *Equip*. Through *Equip*, Pelshaw has taught leadership globally to thousands.

At the onset of The Great Recession Pelshaw became financially over-extended. Coupled with trusting the wrong people and some bad business decisions, Pelshaw suffered a catastrophic loss of a multi-million dollar asset base. In his efforts to stay afloat Pelshaw "robbed Peter to pay Paul" and stupidly, temporarily misused $135,000 of SBA loan proceeds, He was charged with a felony and served a ten-month sentence at Leavenworth Federal Prison Camp. Since serving his time he has focused on consulting, writing, public speaking, and public service. He is also the author of *Raising Up The Champion Within You: David & Goliath Grown-Up Version* and the soon-to-be-released *Time Management is Dead*. Pelshaw and his wife Ilaamen are starting a family.

ALSO BY R.L. PELSHAW:

Raising Up The Champion Within You

Time Management Is Dead
(Coming In 2015)

PART ONE

YOUR NEW LIFE

CHAPTER 1

THE AMERICAN DREAM
(Nightmares are dreams too you know)

The American Dream: to own your own business and not work for "The Man." Unfortunately, some people have turned that dream into a nightmare by starting and operating an illegal business, usually dealing drugs but nearly any illegal business fits into our discussions here. When I use "drug dealer" it also applies to any illegal business. The nightmarish consequences of an illegal business include the great risk, potential violence, impact on families, cost to society, and often prison. To stay away from prison and crime, felons and potential felons need a legal way to support themselves and their families.

Our prisons are filled with ex-drug dealers, most of whom were trying to make a living illegally, and nearly all of whom swear they're never going back to prison or a life of crime. I know this because I met and became friends with many ex-criminals while serving a 10-month sentence at Leavenworth Federal Prison Camp for a white collar crime. In fact, I wrote most of this book while serving my time. My friends in prison gave me invaluable input and feedback, which made this book possible.

According to an important study, as of 2010 there were roughly twenty million living Americans that were incarcerated or ex-offenders, which was projected to be around twenty-four million people as of 2014. Add the families of living ex-prisoners and you have a lot of people directly impacted by incarceration. Include the victims of their crime and you have an even larger number. Add the number of people in criminal enterprise who are not yet felons, and those at risk to offend, and who knows how many millions of people are affected? This is a crisis and something must be done. A report by CNN on December 10, 2013 stated that one in every 108 adult males in the US were currently in jail. To fight a legacy of crime and recidivism we need to create ways current, former, and potential criminals can make money legitimately, but how? I believe showing us how to use our strengths and life skills to be successful in legal businesses will change the destiny of millions.

Internationally renowned speaker and author Bishop T.D. Jakes once said (paraphrased):

> *"The average drug dealer or criminal has the same business skills as the average Fortune 500 C.E.O., or nearly any business owner."*
>
> *-Bishop T.D. Jakes (paraphrased)*

This book is not endorsing drug dealing or any illegal enterprise, but consider this: like any business owner the drug dealer must successfully manage complicated issues. Take a careful look at the following list, you will be surprised by what business skills you already know and are good at:

ISSUES COMMON TO ANY BUSINESS, LEGAL OR ILLEGAL:

Purchasing	Negotiation	Logistics
Shipping	Competition	Sales
Transportation	Security	Pricing
Customer Service	People Skills	Communication
Market Research	Marketing	Promotion
Networking	Solving Problems	Managing Growth
Follow Through	Managing Money	Creating Opportunities
Operations	Staffing	Public Relations
Selecting Vendors	Managing Vendors	Managing Relationships
Payables	Production	Receivables
Collections	Bookkeeping	Storage
Multi-tasking	Innovation	Consistency

Before we go any further write down or highlight the skills above you have already mastered:

_____

_____

Now write down or highlight the skills above you are weakest at:

_____

_____

The items on this list are solid marketable skills in any business enterprise, legal or not. For the "illegal entrepreneur" these skills were learned within illegal enterprise, underground, without police or legal protection, often with great physical danger and the constant threat of loss or violence. Talk about "on the job pressure!" If you can handle that, you're ready to succeed in a legal business. Your key is knowing where to start. In this book I'll help you with that, so continue reading and answering the questions I give you. Then work very hard to discover and do what you learned.

Mastering those listed business skills will make you a success in any business if given the chance. Unfortunately "the system" is stacked against folks with a criminal background. The sad fact is that most employers still discriminate against anyone with a criminal record, even if that means they are violating Federal law. Who's the criminal now? The U.S. Equal Employment Opportunity Commission says that:

> An employer's use of an individual's criminal history in making employment decisions may ... violate the prohibition against employment discrimination under Title VII of the Civil Rights Act of 1964, as amended.

Many criminals and ex-cons don't have formal education or training, and often cannot get jobs earning enough to support themselves or their families. In jail it's not always possible to get education or training beyond a G.E.D., which doesn't prepare them for a well-paying career.

Since it is difficult for ex-cons and others who have operated illegally to get jobs, much less well-paying jobs, it is likely they would return to a life of crime to support themselves and their families.

By not hiring felons could employers be contributing to felons reoffending, or criminals continuing in crime? That's the topic of another book. I've included resources at the end of the book to help felons in their job searches. Please see Appendixes G, H, and I.

Here are some reasons why returning to or continuing in crime is not only a bad idea, but is probably not even feasible anymore:

1. The consequences: jail, fines, loss of assets, impact on reputation, separation from friends and family, and more.

2. If you've done time you're on someone's radar and are likely to be caught again.

3. If marijuana legalization continues, the opportunity for private drug dealers will likely decrease significantly. Legal marijuana trade is now run by legitimate businesses that are licensed and pay taxes on their

operations. Legalization of drugs will not create new drug selling opportunities. It may make the individual illegal drug dealer irrelevant, as increased supply and competition for marijuana sales will drive the price down and most buyers won't risk breaking the law buying when they can buy it legally. "Home grown" cuts out profits for drug dealers altogether. *Here are some reasons why it's a great time to start your own business:*

1.   With Obamacare and pressures from the economy, many employers are cutting back staff to reduce the amount of health insurance they have to buy. These companies will increase outsourcing duties. Globally, outsourcing is the new buzzword and the new normal, with continued long-term growth prospects. You could take advantage of this trend by starting a business that works for companies that outsource. With outsourcing, the employers not only save the overhead of a permanent employee, they save the payroll taxes and benefits, which are an additional $15 - $50/hour on top of the former employees' pay.

2.   For most businesses, a criminal past won't hinder you from having a successful business if you work hard enough and smart enough.

3.   You've been spoiled working for yourself and you probably won't like working for someone else, regardless of the pay.

4.   Your income potential is far greater being self-employed than working a job.

5.   Isn't it time to get away from depending on crime to survive?

Having been successfully self-employed for more than twenty years I have tasted the fruit of being my own boss. I've owned or consulted on business ventures large, small, and growing. These businesses included:

Real Estate Development	Brokerage	Rental Properties
Self-Storage	Hotel/Motels	Sales Organizations
Distributorships	Consulting	Service Businesses
Retail Stores	Health Clubs	Convenience Stores
Restaurants	Grocery Stores	Tool Stores
Pawn Shops	Laundromats	Car Washes
Construction	Thrift Stores	Franchise Businesses
Cleaning Companies	Hair Salons	Barber Shops
Service Businesses	Check Cashing	Trade Schools
Car Lots	Car Detailing	Hair Salons
Art Galleries	Subcontractors	*and more…*

Each of the businesses I worked with had varying degrees of success, and I learned something from each of these businesses. In this book and on the website illegaltolegal.org I hope to convey this knowledge to you, to help you fulfill your dream of being your own boss and legally supporting yourself and your family.

I pray that this book will help you with that process by showing you some of what you need to know to get started on a solid foundation. I also show you nearly 100 businesses you can start for less than $10,000, including thirty-seven businesses you can start for no money! That's in Chapter 4, which contains partial lists of businesses you can start ranging from $0 to more than $100,000.

Part Two contains specific step-by-step examples that I call "Success Snapshots." Instead of writing a boring "how-to" book, or a textbook with a bunch of dry definitions, I decided to use real life examples in a variety of businesses to teach business skills that will help you in whatever business you choose. I encourage you to read all of the examples so that you can learn the ups and downs of each business and possibly find one you're inspired to start.

The Success Snapshots are the stories of actual business owners I interviewed who tell you how they did it. Read all of them: you not only will learn more business skills, but you may discover a business that is a good fit for you.

The website illegaltolegal.org will continue to have more Success Snapshots for you as well. When you have your own "Success Snapshot" send it in and we'll do our best to share it. Maybe you can help someone else on their journey from an illegal life to a legal one.

The Success Snapshots in this book include:

Trucking firm	Martial Arts Studio
Lawn Mowing (just you)	A Lawn Service (w/workers)
Snow Removal	A Laundromat
Housecleaning Service (just you)	Janitorial Service (w/employees)
Being a Personal Trainer	Warehouse Gym/Health Club
U-Haul Dealer (which is free!)	Moving Company
Freelance Graphic Artist	Personal Security Company
Vehicle Detailing Business	Sub-leasing rental real estate
Rental Business	Being a Subcontractor
Pawn Shop	Mobile Home Rentals
Becoming an Energy Auditor	The Pusher

Part Three contains the Business Plan Checklist ™, forms, and other free tools to help you regardless what business you want to start or buy. There are more free tools for you at our website illegaltolegal.org.

My goal is to give you helpful information, without useless fluff but in an inspirational, motivating way. Use the book to learn, to be an ongoing reference, and to help guide you to start your new business and life.

It would be hard for me, or anyone accustomed to running their own business, to find a job with the same freedom, income, challenges, or responsibilities that I have working for myself. I love the "rush" of calling my own shots and "rolling the dice" on deals and business ventures.

Have you ever wondered why 75 percent of ex-cons reoffend within five years of prison release? I don't think it's because of uncontrollable urges to commit crime. A lack of a viable income source or no vision to earn a living without crime are reasons many ex-offenders or potential felons turn to crime. This is in spite of their promise to never go back to prison. Something radical and drastic must be done to break the vicious circle that has created "inmate nation."

This book was created because I believe if you operated an illegal business you can be very successful in a legitimate business _if_ you take the lessons you've learned from your past and apply them to your future. You don't need a business degree. You already have one! STREET UNIVERSITY is what your diploma says! There is no shame in that. In fact, you should use that to your advantage. If you have formal education that's great! I not only want to give you hope that you can start a business, I also want to bring you the vision and show a path for it.

Several of my friends in prison told me they would've gone into a legitimate business, but they had no idea what to do. Together, we will help find what's good for you, but it all depends on your choices and efforts going forward.

Starting your own business may not be as easy for you as going back to illegal business, but it's worth the effort to avoid prison and prove to the world that you can make it. It may not be the "crazy money" you quickly made doing something illegal, but with your own business you can sleep at night without worrying that you'll be caught, or if someone will take you out. You've worked hard for everyone else, and what do you have to show for it? Now is the time for you to step out and do something for yourself.

An old proverb says "the journey of a thousand miles begins with a single step." Whether you're still in a life of crime or trying to avoid going back to it, you may be thinking: "Great! I'd love to own my business, but how do I get started?" My answer to you has four parts:

1. Your strengths: We will help discover them and refocus them on your new venture.

2. Your passions: Uncovering these will help reveal business possibilities for you.

3. The foundation: We will give you what you need to get started on this journey.

4. The path: We will give you a checklist and specific examples to help show you the way.

The rich and wise King Solomon said in the book of Ecclesiastes that "He that regards the wind will not sow; he that regards the clouds will not reap." What does that mean? It means we cannot, and must not, wait for perfect conditions but we must do whatever we can, whenever we can, with whatever we have.

There will be those who will say that people need much more information before they start a business. It's true, you can and should always get as much information and training as you can. We should be lifelong learners and always try to improve ourselves and learn something new every day. You're doing that already by reading this book.

Many books have been written about business, but you'll never start a business if you wait to read all those books first. Besides, you have a business degree from Street University and most people desperately need a legal source of income right now. You will learn along the way, but you have to get started. I don't attempt to erase the need for more study. That's why I will continually update the website and write useful material to help you make your own "Success Snapshot."

I pray this book spurs you to further action. It's intended to help you to look back at your experiences, success, and failures, and use those elements to propel you into successful self-employment. I also hope you keep learning and growing along the way.

The next two chapters will help answer the "strengths" and "passions" portions of your journey, while the rest of the book will help provide you with a good foundation and path to get you started. If you are currently incarcerated you know that you cannot start or conduct business, but you obviously can use your time to learn, prepare, and plan for a new future. Let's begin the journey!

CHAPTER 2

WHAT ARE MY STRENGTHS AND HOW CAN I USE THEM?

Have you ever thought about what your strengths are? That's like me asking you "what are you really good at?" *Other* than something illegal! Your strengths are those actions that not only come easy to you, but also give you the greatest or best results.

Since your strengths give you the best return on your investments of time, talent, and treasure, focus on them and stay away from your weaknesses. Have someone else do those things you don't do well while you focus on what you are productive in: that's an important key to success and happiness.

Your strengths are the areas you know and love the most. My challenge with this book is to convince you that it wasn't the illegal business you knew and loved the most; it was owning your own business that you knew and loved the most. It was the joy of working in your strengths that you enjoyed. You're already entrepreneurial, a hard worker, a self-starter, and a risk taker. These are all keys to building a successful business.

With this book I'm showing you how to get back into business for yourself, legally. Can you envision a successful business that supports you and your family and keeps you out of jail? Starting a business isn't easy, but it's easier than making money illegally when you factor the risks and consequences of it. If you've done time then you already have the patience and perseverance needed to be successful in a new business. No matter what your challenges are in starting in a business, all of them are easier than being away from your family, while your kids grow up without you and your friends and family forget about you. Starting and running a business is easier than being in prison, even if the money isn't as lucrative or as fast as illegal income. When you run a legal business you still get to be your own boss but without the risk of being arrested, beat up, or killed.

You can succeed at any business you want as long as you focus on your strengths and do something you love (are passionate about). Of course once you find what you want to do, you must be willing to work hard and stick with it without giving up. An important key to success in life, according to author and humorist Mark Twain, is making "your vocation a vacation." Finding what your strengths are is part of the process of getting you ready to own and operate your own legal business.

Your strengths are found in your past, both good and bad. But I'm not here to beat you up over what you did, or might even be doing now. I'm here to give you a practical path that you can follow to help you use your past to propel you to a new future, your destiny, a future where you own a legal business and you have left the criminal world behind.

Take a moment and think about the Space Shuttle. Obviously the Shuttle was not designed to stay on earth. It fulfills its destiny in the stars, not on the launch pad.

What is the biggest obstacle the Shuttle must overcome to get into space? It's not gravity but the weight of the fuel. The fuel weighs more than nineteen times what the Shuttle weighs. It's ironic because the Shuttle needs the fuel to get into orbit, but the fuel is so heavy it becomes the biggest obstacle the Shuttle must overcome to blast into space. Breaking through the atmosphere into its destiny is the most difficult thing the Shuttle will ever do.

I promised to show you how to use your past to propel you to your destiny. Pretend you are the Space Shuttle. You're designed and destined to be high above where you are now, but you're stuck on earth. You're on the launch pad, ready for something to get you moving. You are yearning for something better, knowing you don't belong where you are now. You are unhappy that you can't get to where you want to be but you don't know how to reach the stars.

As the Shuttle you have to use your fuel to blast off, but what is your fuel? My friend, it's not dealing drugs or any other type of illegal business with all of its horrible consequences. You want to blast away from that life. But how?

Your past, your life experience, is like the fuel in the Space Shuttle. If the fuel is properly used it can propel you into orbit, your destiny. If the fuel is improperly used it becomes dangerous, explosive, and can destroy the Shuttle. If the fuel is unused it weighs you down and keeps you stuck on the launch pad. Life on the launch pad is an unfilled life. On the launch pad you're never going anywhere, never changing, never doing anything differently, never improving, and never learning. All you are doing is wasting away and decaying while you ignore your destiny above you.

You must decide if you want to let your past weigh you down, destroy you, or propel you to your destiny among the stars. What will you decide? Are you willing to do what it takes to make it legitimately, so you can reach your destiny, the life you were meant to live? Once the Shuttle blasts off it cannot return to Earth until its mission is complete. A return mid-launch would be catastrophic for the Shuttle.

History gives us another example of the commitment required for success. Spanish explorer Hernan Cortez burned his ships when he reached the New World in the 1500s. You must have that level of commitment if you wish to reach your goal. Returning to the past should not be an option at all no matter how hard it is to launch or break through to your destiny. Just as the Space Shuttle cannot return to earth mid-launch, and there were no ships for Cortez' men to return to Spain, there should be no chance of you ever returning to a life of crime. <u>Close that door forever!</u> This book will show you ways to start your own business so you don't have to return to or continue crime to make a living.

Look again at that list of Business Skills in Chapter 1, reprinted below:

Purchasing	Negotiation	Logistics
Shipping	Competition	Sales
Transportation	Security	Pricing
Customer Service	People Skills	Communication
Market Research	Marketing	Promotion
Networking	Solving Problems	Managing Growth
Follow Through	Managing Money	Creating Opportunities
Operations	Staffing	Public Relations
Selecting Vendors	Managing Vendors	Managing Relationships
Payables	Production	Receivables
Collections	Bookkeeping	Storage
Multi-tasking	Innovation	Consistency

What on that list are you really good at?

_____

_____

I'm good at three things: Communicating, Creating Opportunities, and Solving Problems. Since those are my strengths I focus on skills that allow me to use those strengths. Doing so makes me much fulfilled and usually very successful.

What type of work makes you very happy? For example, is it dealing with people or working with numbers? Could it be reading reports or working with your hands? Sales? Production? Please write down the type of activities that make you happy:

_____

_____

What are you really good at? Maybe your strength(s) is not on that list. Before we proceed forward take the time to list your strengths here:

_____

_____

For every strength that you wrote down, also write down an example of how you used that strength in your life and what it gained you:

_____

_____

_____

Go back to the list above where you wrote down the activities that made you happy. Compare that list to the list of your strengths. Is there any way to incorporate the two together? If so, how?

_____

_____

_____

Now let's do something very important. I'm going to prove to you that you have the skills to start a successful legitimate business. Think back on your "illegal entrepreneurism" and answer these questions below:

1. How did you start your illegal business?

2. Did you have a mentor, or an advisor? If so, how did they help you?

3. Did you do it part-time or full-time?

4. Were you working a job while it was starting off?

5. How did you promote it?

6. Did you have much "word of mouth" business? Why or why not?

7. Why did people do business with you instead of your competition?

8. Would you consider yourself a professional? Did you act professionally? Why or why not?

9. How did you deal with your competition?

10. Did you do business the same way as your competition or was it different than them? If it was different, what were the differences between you and your competitor's business?

11. Did you provide better service? How? Please be specific. This may be the key to your gaining and keeping new customers.

12. Were you more or less expensive than your competitors?

13. Did your customers care about your price?

14. Was your product better or worse? Why?

15. How often did you check the prices of your competition?

16. How did you know what to charge?

17. How often, and why, did you adjust your prices?

18. How did you operate your business, by yourself or with staff?

19. What did you do to keep books or accounts?

20. How much of your profits did you reinvest in the business?

21. Did you leave enough for yourself to live on?

22. How long after you started it were you able to start using some of the profits on yourself?

23. Did you spend your profits wisely?

24. How were you unwise in your spending?

Hopefully you are starting to see that you have legitimate business skills. The questions we just went through are the same questions you will have to answer when you launch your new legal business. With that in mind please answer these last questions:

1. What were the keys to your success?

2. What did you do uniquely well, or better than anyone else?

3. If money was no object, and in a "perfect world," what would you do for a living if given the chance?

4. What business(es) are there that can use your strengths? Your skills? Your past experience?

5. Once you get back into a business for yourself, what would you do differently? "Not getting caught" is not an acceptable answer! Be as specific as you can. The more you think about this question the better prepared and better motivated you can be to get ready to start your new venture.

6. What are your weaknesses? For instance, I understand bookkeeping, but you do not want me doing your books! I believe I can do almost anything, but the truth be known when it comes to bookkeeping I don't have the passion, temperament, or expertise for it. So bookkeeping is a weakness of mine. I'm not productive when I am wasting time on my weaknesses. Always focus on your strengths and someone passionate and gifted in the areas of your weakness.

Please list some of your weaknesses below:

_____

_____

You can't avoid your weaknesses altogether. When starting a business you are required to fulfill many roles, some of which may fall into areas you are not passionate about or may not be your primary strengths. Knowing what your weaknesses are helps you to manage them. Have a plan to deal with them when those instances occur that exposes you to them. Remember also, sometimes we do need to work on the weakness that weakens you.

An effective strategy for dealing with weaknesses is to ask yourself: are your goals being best served by you working in the area of your weakness, and do you have the opportunity to let someone else do that task for you so you can focus on your strengths? Sometimes you must even do tasks within your weakness, but try to minimize those times and work through them as quickly as possible when you face them.

For more on strengths and weaknesses, I highly recommend you buy the book *Strengthsfinder 2.0* by the Gallup Organization. Strengthsfinder is a powerful tool that will surprise you and reveal your strengths. This focus will help you be the most productive and avoid unproductive actions. You will be surprised how much you learn about yourself from taking the twenty minute +/- test.

Now that we've discovered your strengths and weaknesses let's discuss your passions, and learn how that can help you find a business to start that blends your strengths and passions.

CHAPTER 3

TURNING YOUR PASSIONS INTO A BUSINESS

In the last chapter we identified some of your strengths and now we want to find out your passions. What we mean by "passions" has nothing to do with romance, but has everything to do with what you love doing. Who wants to make a living and be miserable? You can get a job for that! Studies--and common sense--indicate you will earn the most money and be the most successful doing something you are passionate about. It has been said if you love your work it is never really like work.

Dave Ramsey, best-selling author and personal finance expert, says studies indicate 85 percent of financial success comes from your passion and integrity, while only 15 percent of your success comes from formal study or training. Your degree from Street University is looking pretty good now, isn't it?

Do you know what your passions are? If so you are very blessed, and you can focus on a business that uses your passions. Your passion excites you. It motivates you and gives you energy. Passion can overcome a lack of resources. Your passions make you happy. Your passions make you mad, and drive you to get involved. Your passions make you laugh, and you think about your passions a lot. You can excel at a task that uses your passion because doing it always feels right.

Passions are not just talent. You can be talented in numerous areas but maybe only passionate about a few things. Your passions will multiply your talents and strengths, but your talents and strengths might not necessarily be your passions. People might see you as being very talented in an area you're passionate about so they ask your advice or help with it. These are all symptoms of what your passions may be.

Don't you enjoy hanging around people who have found and are living in their passion? Don't you like doing business with someone who is passionate about serving you and getting you the best product for your money? Don't you trust someone more who is passionate about what they do? Why can't you be that business owner who is passionate about their work?

Restaurants are a great example of passions in action in business. Who do you think is more passionate, tries harder, and gives a better product? A food cart vendor selling food he made from his own recipes, or a worker at a fast food restaurant?

So what is your passion? Here's a partial list of some passions, please look it over. It is meant to help you see examples of passions, and get you thinking about what your passion is. Notice I said what your passions "is" and not what your passions "are." You may be passionate or talented at numerous things, but I want you to try to find the top thing you are most passionate about. Finding your top passion and making it into a business is the key to your success and a happy future.

A Partial List of Passions:
- Buying and selling things such as: cars, comic books, coins, stamps, dolls, art, etc.

- Repairing or restoring vehicles: cars, trucks, motorcycles, boats, RV's, trailers.

Also:

Working with your hands	Working outside
Mechanics or Repairing things	Travel, Outfitting
Making things grow	Animals
Lawn care	Cleaning
Dealing with people	Coaching or Consulting
Writing, Research	Security
Woodworking	Hunting, Fishing, Boating
Working with the elderly	Building things
Painting	Gaming
Helping Others	Clothing or Jewelry
Decorating	Home Improvement
Cycling	Real Estate
Technology or Computers	Working out
Audio Equipment or Electronics	Cooking

You might be saying "I don't need a passion. I need an income!" All things considered wouldn't you rather have a business you can enjoy instead of one you just make money at? You'll make the most money doing something you enjoy and believe in. You can make money at a lot of things, but not everything will make you happy.

Motivational speaker and author the late Zig Ziglar says "if you want to find your passion in an occupation or career find that one thing you love so much you would do it for free and make that your career." That's what the earlier Mark Twain quote meant by "make your vocation a vacation."

Nearly anything can be a passion. Maybe yours wasn't on that list. What are you passionate about?

Sometimes your passion will lead you to where there is an unmet need or something that needs to be fixed. Mary Kay Ash was a gifted saleswoman who lived in an age where there were limited opportunities for women in business. Despite opposition from society and limited funds Mary Kay started a company that has made tremendous business opportunities for hundreds of thousands of women, all while providing great cosmetics. From her initial investment of $5,000 she built a multi-billion dollar enterprise.

Has anyone else ever made their passions into a business? Sure they have! Henry Ford, King's Hawaiian Bakery, Papa John's Pizza, Facebook, Southwest Airlines, FedEx, McDonald's – those are a few of the many companies that were birthed with a passion. We know about the huge success stories, but every business that was started that provides a good product or service and is passionate about it, is a success story. The truth be known you will need passion in your business to propel you through the hard times.

I'm sure you can think of at least one or two examples of people who have turned what they love into a business. What do you know about that business? How did it start (if you know)? Was it operated out of a home, an office, a store, or a shop? What tools and equipment did it require? Did it require any special licensing or registrations? Did it have any employees?

Can you picture yourself doing that same business or a business that revolves around your passions? What is it? What does it look like?

Often our passions involve our strengths, but not always. To be the most productive, we should find a way to connect your strengths with your passions.

Here's an example to help you connect your strengths with your passions. Suppose you love cars and have a strong attention to detail. If you could combine those two, you likely would be very successful at that business. You could start a car detailing business, either at a shop or a mobile detailing service, and combine your love for cars with your attention to detail. Or if you have the skill and tools, you can start a mechanic shop, even a mobile mechanic service. If you applied yourself to it, ran it right, built the business, promoted it, earned referral and repeat business you likely will gain a reputation for being the best detailer or the best mechanic there is. People will pay top dollar for the best.

Remember the questions I asked you to answer in Chapter 2:

1. If money was no object, and in a "perfect world" what would you do for a living if given the chance?

2. Is there a business that you can use your strengths at? Your skills? Your past experiences? If so what?

Do the answers to the two questions above match or are they two different things? If they match, you're on the right track. If they're different, is one of the answers to the questions above something you can realistically attempt? For instance, you may have a great pizza recipe, and your dream is to your own restaurant. At this moment in time you don't have enough money to open your new restaurant, and your job doesn't pay enough to help save money to open one either. What's wrong with renting a food truck to sell pizzas from after work, then save the profits until you can open your own restaurant? That's exactly what a friend of mine did.

Thinking about your answer to Question 2 above, what businesses can you think of that use your passions and strengths? Rank them from 1-10 (from easy start-up to difficult start-up) and state your answer below:

_____

_____

How do they use your strengths and your passions?

Keep in mind, if your ultimate goal is to be a NASCAR driver, there's nothing wrong with starting a mobile mechanic business. You can grow that business into a car repair shop. Use the profits from your shop to gradually get what you need to race. Or build up the shop and make it successful enough to sell for a lot of money which could fund your NASCAR dream.

To put it another way, author and speaker Zig Ziglar says "do not let what you cannot do interfere with what you can do."

The next chapter contains lists of businesses with start-up costs from $0 on up. Feel free to skip ahead and see if any of those businesses might inspire your passion and possibilities. Even if you haven't narrowed it down to just one, the rest of the book will help show you different paths and different tools you can use to be successful in your own business. Let's continue the journey!

CHAPTER 4

BUSINESSES TO START FROM $0 +

America was built on small businesses. Even today small businesses are the greatest employment engine generating 65 percent of all new jobs created between 1993 and 2009. According to the U.S. Department of Commerce 99.7 percent of all private employers are small businesses, defined as companies with less than 500 employees.

I became self-employed because even with my college degree I couldn't get a decent job. Small businesses continue to provide the most jobs in our economy. I am convinced the health of our society and country as a whole is tied to the success of small businesses, our ethic of hard work, and our ability to innovate and solve problems.

Many of my friends in prison told me they would've started a business and left crime but they had no idea what business to get into. To inspire and motivate you I've made a list of over 160 potential businesses, thirty-seven of them with ZERO start-up costs, the rest ranging all the way up to $100,000 +. Hopefully these lists will inspire you to action. Check the website illegaltolegal.org for an up-to-date list.

Of course, these estimated amounts are just the bare minimums of start-up investment and your actual costs will likely be different than these beginning general estimates. You can always invest more money in a business if you want to. Also, these estimates assume you start the business by yourself with minimal or no payroll.

The purpose of these estimates is to give a starting point of what your bare minimum start-up costs could be. These will vary widely depending on the scope of your vision, how you implement it, what your living expenses/overhead are, and whether you have a job or other source of income while you launch your venture.

I also assume you will continually invest in your business after start-up to grow your business, which is an additional expense that I do not factor here. I also assume that you will have a vehicle, a computer, and a decent smartphone that can text and send emails. These items aren't required but they are a good base to start from. I did not factor their cost into the start-up estimates below.

At illegaltolegal.org and in the next chapter there are free features to help you estimate the actual start-up costs for a business you may start, as well as other tools to help you launch your new venture. Please let us know how the list and tools we provide worked, and if you have any suggestions or changes that could help others in the future. As ex-felons/criminals we need to help each other succeed. We can do this by giving each other advice, and referring business to each other.

There is no lack of success stories of businesses that started with more passion than money:

Duck Dynasty

Google

WhatsApp

Steve Jobs and Apple Computers (from a garage)

Colonel Sanders and Kentucky Fried Chicken (KFC)

Truett Cathy and Chick-Fil-A

FUBU

Nike

Plus thousands of small businesses you don't even know about that you see and use regularly! Even Walmart was once a small business.

You may not launch a multi-billion dollar business. You don't need that to be successful. Making a decent living without returning to crime is a great success. Perhaps owning a business is a way for you to accomplish that.

Don't let a lack of funds stop you from starting your own business. How much money did you start your illegal enterprise with? Like most businesses you probably started small, reinvested your earnings, and built your business. You know how to do that, now do it again with something legitimate. Even if you have to work a job and launch your business part time, that is better than not trying anything and being like the Space Shuttle stuck on the launch pad.

No matter how bleak your circumstances are you can always start small and grow instead of returning to crime. Remember that verse in Ecclesiastes that cautions us to not wait for perfect conditions. The advantage of starting small is it allows you time to work out the bugs in your new venture, and helps you build a solid foundation for growth.

When starting a business you can never have enough available cash on hand. In business lingo this is called "working capital." How much working capital is enough? As much as you can get. Having six months of overhead and living expenses is ideal, but not required. As far as working capital goes, do the best you can, and be very careful spending money until you have built up the business and have some cash on hand for a rainy day. Remember: it always rains and never when you want it to! Once you start to earn money your first goal should be to set aside that amount of money that covers your six months of overhead and living expense.

If you are working a job while you are launching a business your working capital requirements could be less. Working a job can give you valuable experience and contacts in a field, as well as a list of potential new customers. Some businesses may require your full time effort, and you may not be able to work a side job. Unless you have the resources to do otherwise I always advise you to work a job if you can until the income from your new business is enough to let your survive. You've hustled before, get your hustle on now and muster the effort to launch your new life.

Great news: there are nearly 100 businesses listed here that you can start for less than $10,000. Maybe you can think of a business that should be on these lists. If so, please let us know on the website. I've organized the businesses based on their estimated minimum costs to start. These are estimates only and you should carefully plan and make your own budget before you launch out. Don't let the amount of capital required dictate which business to select. Find the business that uses your passion and strengths, then work from there.

Some businesses I listed in more than one category (like cleaning, lawn care, contracting) depending on whether you are working it yourself or you start with employees. If you buy a successful well established cleaning service you could easily pay several hundred thousand dollars for it. Again, the investment depends on your resources and vision for what business you want. You can start small to reinvest your earnings in advertising, equipment and the tools you need to grow bigger. These lists are not laws. They are guidelines to help get you started on your dream. Don't let what you don't have keep you from trying something.

Several of the businesses on this list require licensing, training, or special skills. You may have to go back to school, but if you have the skills or training you need that's great! If not, go to work for a company that is doing what you want to do, and learn from them while you work towards getting licensed, trained, and experienced. Some companies will pay for your licensing and training. Pick your boss' brain continually and try to learn something new every day. You never know, if you impress your boss they may work out a scenario where they eventually sell you their business. You'd be surprised to know how often that actually happens, but only to those who have gone above and beyond the normal call of duty at work.

Don't try to do multiple types of businesses until you have established one that pays your bills and gives you a solid foundation. There are strengths and weaknesses as well as pros and cons associated with every business. Hopefully you connect with something on the lists. Perhaps the business you envision was not on the lists. No matter. The important thing is for you to decide on a business you want to start based on your strengths, weaknesses, and passions.

Be open to all possibilities, and look at existing businesses that may be for sale. You may be able to get a better deal buying an existing business than starting that same business from scratch. There's no shortage of businesses with motivated sellers: salons, laundromats, restaurants, construction companies, you name it. A good website to look at if you are interested in acquiring an existing business or franchise is bizbuysell.com/.

Ask if the seller would finance the purchase. What's wrong with using the profits you generate from your new business to pay for the business itself? Some businesses are for sale for health reasons, or they are owned by an older person with no heirs or family to take over. Others may have run into difficulty. I have acquired troubled businesses and did well with them, just make sure you don't pay too much money for them. Before you buy it make sure you know exactly why the business is in trouble, and make sure you can fix that problem before you invest.

The rest of this chapter is devoted to 165 different businesses you can start based on the following estimated start-up costs:

$0 - $1,000
$1,000 - $10,000
$10,000 - $20,000
$20,000 - $100,000
Over $100,000

When reading the lists an * means that business is profiled as a Success Snapshot in Part 2 of this book. Check the website illegaltolegal.org for more Success Snapshots. Let us know if you think of a business that should be on the list, or if you want to share your story. We welcome your input.

Business Start-ups
From $0 – $1000

- App Developer
- Blogger
- Bookkeeping Service
- Booth Rental:
  Applies to a Barber/Stylist, Nail Tech, Tattoo Artist
- Booth at a Flea Market/Swap Meet:
  (vintage items, DVDs, books, arts & crafts, etc.)
- Build Rock Walls, Retaining Walls, etc.
- Buy/Sell Things on Craigslist, EBay, Auctions, etc.
- Caulking Subcontractor
- Chimney Sweep
- Cleaning Gutters
- Cleaning Service* (without employees)
- Club Promoter
- Consultant
- Contractor or Subcontractor* (without employees)
- Create an E-zine
- Counseling Service
- Deck Building, Repair, Washing, or Staining
- Detailing Business:
  For Autos, Boats, RV's, Motorcycles, Airplanes, Trucks*
- Dog Waste Clean-up (easily make $75/hour)
- Event Planner or Promoter
- Furnace Filter Changing Service
- Gardening Services: Service People's Flowerbeds and Bushes
- Gutter Cleaning Subcontractor
- Handyman (if you already own your tools, or rent as needed)
- House-Sitting
- Landscaper (without employees)
- Lawn Mowing (without employees)*
- Massage Therapist:
  (lease space in a salon, chiropractor's office, health club)
- Painting Company (without employees)
- Personal Trainer* (easily earn $50-150/hour +)
- Personal Shopper / Assistant / Personal Chef
- Pet Sitting, Pet Walking, Pet Training
- Translator (both documents and in person)
- Upholstery Business (home based)
- Website designer
- Window Cleaning business

*There is a Success Snapshot
for this item.

BUSINESS START-UPS
FROM $0 - $1000

- App Developer
- Blogger
- Bookkeeping Service
- Booth Rental:
  Applies to a Barber/Stylist, Nail Tech, Tattoo Artist
- Booth at a Flea Market/Swap Meet:
  (vintage items, DVDs, books, arts & crafts, etc.)
- Build Rock Walls, Retaining Walls, etc.
- Buy/Sell Things on Craigslist, EBay, Auctions, etc.
- Caulking Subcontractor
- Chimney Sweep
- Cleaning Gutters
- Cleaning Service* (without employees)
- Club Promoter
- Consultant
- Contractor or Subcontractor* (without employees)
- Create an E-zine
- Counseling Service
- Deck Building, Repair, Washing, or Staining
- Detailing Business: For Autos, Boats, RV's, Motorcycles, Airplanes, Trucks*
- Dog Waste Clean-up (easily make $75/hour)
- Event Planner or Promoter
- Furnace Filter Changing Service
- Gardening Services: Service People's Flowerbeds and Bushes
- Gutter Cleaning Subcontractor
- Handyman (if you already own your tools, or rent as needed)
- Home Daycare
- House-Sitting
- Landscaper (without employees)
- Lawn Mowing (without employees)*
- Massage Therapist:
  (lease space in a salon, chiropractor's office, health club)
- Painting Company (without employees)
- Personal Trainer* (easily earn $50-150/hour +)
- Personal Shopper / Assistant / Personal Chef
- Pet Sitting, Pet Walking, Pet Training
- Translator (both documents and in person)
- Upholstery Business (home based)
- Website designer
- Window Cleaning business

*There is a Success Snapshot
for this item.

Business Start-ups
From $10k - $20k

Any of the businesses from the previous two lists can be added to this category
if you start with employees or a rented location (like a shop or office).

The best extra investment you can make when starting a business
is good advertising and promotion.

- Auto Repair Business
- Barber Shop / Hairstylist Salon
- Nail Salon
- Catering Business
- Computer Repair Shop
- Consignment Store
  (sell other people's products on consignment: clothes, tools, furniture, etc.)
- Delivery Business
- DJ Business (with equipment you own)
- Electronics Repair Shop
- Flower Shop
- Food Cart
- Martial Arts Studio*
  (you can start for less than $1k)
- Manufacturer's Representative
- Massage Therapy Salon
- Mobile Home Rentals*
- Motorcycle Accessories Shop
- Motorcycle Repair Shop
- Photography / Video Business
- Sand Blasting Subcontractor
- Upholstery Shop
- Towing Business
- Wheels and Rims Shop
- Woodworking Shop
- Worm Farm
  (you can make over $100,000/year on this if you work it right)

*There is a Success Snapshot
for this item.

BUSINESS START-UPS FROM $20K - $100K

Other than acquiring an existing business in this price category
here are more options for you:

- Art Gallery / Artist Collective
- Audio Shop (car or home)
- Auto Accessories / Customization Shop
- Auto Body Shop
- Butcher Shop
- Buying / Selling Surplus Government Items
- Catering Business
- Clothing Store
- Coffee Shop
- Comic Book Store
- Day Spa
- Delivery Business
- Fireworks Stand
- Framing Shop
- Hip Hop / Gospel Music Store
- Janitorial Company*
- Landscaper (with employees)
- Laundromat*
- Lawn Service*
- Moving Business (owned equipment)
- Nail Shop, From Scratch
- Piercing Shop, From Scratch
- Procurement Agent
- Rental Property Through Subletting It Out in Smaller Chunks to Tenants*
- Small Restaurant, Sandwich Shop (taking over an existing operation)
- Servicing Fire Extinguishers
- Solar Panel Distributor / Contractor
- Tattoo Shop, From Scratch
- Tobacco Shop
- Used Book Store
- Used CD / Record / Game Store
- Used Furniture Shop
- Used Tire shop
- Vending Route
- Vintage and Thrift Store
- Warehouse Gym*
- Wholesale Artificial Flower Business
- Wind Turbine Distributor / Contractor

*There is a Success Snapshot
for this item.*

BUSINESS START-UPS FROM $100K ON UP

There are a lot of businesses you can buy for $100,000 and up.
Space does not allow me to list them all. Here are a few to help inspire you:

- Antique Store
- Auction Business
- Auto Body Shop (buying an existing one)
- Bakery
- Bed and Breakfast
- Boarding House
- Car Lot
- Car Repair Shop
- Car Wash
- Check Cashing Business / Payday Loan Business
- Daycare Center
- Ethnic Food Store or Grocery Store
- Flea Market / Swap Meet
- Flipping Houses
- Franchise Business
- General Contractor
- Glass Business
- Grading Contractor
- Gym / Health Club*
- Hotel / Motel
- Import / Export Business (if you have or can get international contacts)
- Import Shop
- Import / Export Business
- Jewelry Store
- Laundromat or Dry Cleaner (buy an existing or open a larger operartion)
- Mortuary / Funeral Home
- Oil Change Shop
- Pawn Shop (no guns if you have a criminal record)
- Rental Business* (tools, equipment, skis, party supplies, etc.)
- Rental Hall
- Rental Properties
- Salvage Business
- Sit Down Restaurant
- Small Restaurant, Sandwich shop (buy an existing or open a larger operartion)
- Storage Lot; Self Storage Business
- Tire Shop
- Trade School
- Trucking Company, Multiple Trucks*

*There is a Success Snapshot for this item.

Did you find anything on the lists that matched your strengths and passions? Was there anything you can picture yourself doing, or is your new business something that is not on those lists?

Whether you found your business on the lists or not, the rest of the book will give you valuable information to prepare you to launch and succeed in whatever new business you chose. The next chapter will help you plan and implement your new business.

CHAPTER 5

FAILING TO PLAN IS PLANNING TO FAIL:
START WITH THE END IN MIND

> *"You were born to win, but to be the winner you were born to be, you must PLAN to win, PREPARE to win, and EXPECT to win."*
>
> *-Zig Ziglar*

Why do I need "planning" for my business? Isn't working hard enough? I know what I'm going to do, I just need to go do it, so how will planning help?

Who builds a house without a plan? Don't you have a plan when you go on vacation? It amazes me how many people will risk their life savings and their career on starting a business without a plan.

Will you need money for your new business? Many banks won't lend money without a business plan. The government won't give grants without a plan. Most investors won't invest without a plan. The best employees won't work for a leader without a plan. Even friends and family will be reluctant to give you help without a plan.

But there's one reason for planning even more important than all of the others combined. The great Hall of Fame College Basketball Coach John Wooden said it best:

> *"When opportunity arises, it's too late to prepare."*
>
> *-John Wooden*

You must plan for the success you want to achieve. Have you ever heard the story of the two lumberjacks that bet each other over who could chop down the most trees in a day? The first lumberjack immediately set about chopping down trees, while the second one spent the whole morning sharpening his axe. By the end of the day, the lumberjack that prepared his axe won the bet, by a great margin!

Simply put, you need to plan to handle the success you want to achieve. When you don't plan you don't activate the wonderful process of preparation. The process of preparation will make you think of things you hadn't considered. It will give you ideas, reveal solutions, and let you know of potential problems.

What happens when you're unprepared? Usually lost opportunity or disaster. Failing to plan is planning to fail.

You're ready to start your new business and leave a life of crime, but how? Start with the end in mind. Knowing what you want your business to be is the "end" result we are looking for here. What is your vision for your business? What goals do you have for your business? Other than making a lot of money of course.

Author and motivational speaker Tony Robbins says "Setting goals is the first step in turning the invisible into the visible." I am asking you to think about the goals for what you want your business to be. Answering this question is more detailed than just setting a goal for how much money you want to make. This chapter will help.

Think about the "big picture" and try to be as focused as you can. It's a tough question to answer, and you probably won't get it right in just one attempt. The answers to this question will adjust as you proceed with planning and working toward your goal. When I'm planning a new venture I like to start with a vision of what I want the business to be, then work backwards from there to figure out the steps needed to launch the new enterprise. That is starting with the end in mind.

Planning is the key to your business success. Hard work is good, but hard work alone is not enough. We need to work smarter, not harder. The way to work smarter is daily and long term planning. Internationally acclaimed author and leadership expert Dr. John C. Maxwell says that "twenty minutes of planning will save two hours of work."

> *"20 minutes of planning will save you 2 hours of work."*
> -Dr. John C. Maxwell

You should plan ahead for the business you want to build and daily plan your day, in writing, before you start your day. Do it enough and it will become a habit for you that will help you achieve and maintain success. My upcoming book *Time Management is Dead* gives practical strategies to help you manage your priorities, maximize your productivity, and achieve your goals.

Currently, 49 percent of new businesses don't survive more than five years. I personally believe much of the failure rate is due to a lack of planning. The good news is that 70 percent of new businesses survive at least two years, so the odds are good that you can succeed. This chapter is devoted to helping you plan and prepare to be in the percentage of new businesses that not only survive, but thrive because they were prepared for it.

We've all had distractions, interruptions, emergencies and problems that have derailed our best intentions. Planning helps you reduce these and gives a way to deal with them when they occur. You have a lot riding on your ability to make your business work, so why not give yourself as many tools as you can to help you succeed? Planning requires some time and effort. Aren't you and your future worth that? It doesn't matter if you know how to plan. I will show you how to get started here in this book, on the website, and in other books I will be publishing.

Planning may even be the difference between success and failure in your new business. A business plan should map out the path to the Who, What, Where, Why, When, and How of your business. It should tell the story of your vision in a convincing way, with proof to support your idea. In a perfect world you would think about what exactly you want your new business to be, and then make a plan to list and organize all of the steps and items needed to get there.

I've written many business plans. Plans can range from five to 150 pages, although the majority are around twenty pages long. I've included a sample of a business plan in Part 3, Appendix B and on our website illegaltolegal.org. We also offer a service to write custom business plans for you.

Unfortunately, most business plans are written and never looked at again, even though when properly written and used they become an invaluable tool.

I'm not against business plans. I'm against business plans that aren't useful to you. The best written, most detailed plan means nothing if you don't refer to it often to help keep you on track.

I personally think you need to plan extensively but for most businesses you may not need a complicated full-blown business plan to start your business. You need to generate legitimate income as quickly as possible so you can afford to avoid the life of crime.

For the quickest results I've developed a checklist to help you plan your business. I call it the Business Plan Checklist ™. I have one in this book at the end of this chapter, and as a form in Part 3 of this Book, Appendix A, and through illegaltolegal.org. For a reasonable fee we can help you to make a custom Business Plan Checklist™ for you if desired.

Before you attempt a business plan I suggest you start with the Business Plan Checklist™. Using the Business Plan Checklist™ should help you get your business started sooner. When you are able, you should do a business plan. Whether you do a full business plan or not, the Checklist is a powerful tool to help you.

The Business Plan Checklist™ is a listing of many of the items you need to be aware of, provide for, and plan for as you start, operate, and grow your business. This is simply a starting point which will change over time. The Business Plan Checklist™ is designed to give you a practical tool you can use to get you started now and achieve the results of a business plan without necessarily having to write a complete one.

While working with the Business Plan Checklist™ you will think of specific areas that apply to your vision and situation, and you can add those elements to your Business Plan Checklist™. If you want to write a business plan, you can use the Checklist as a starting point to build a written plan around, whether you do it yourself or we help you with it. You can also schedule a private over-the-phone business coaching session where we work with you to complete a customized Business Plan Checklist™.

After this book achieves 100,000 units sold, I will hold a competition to judge the best business plans/Business Plan Checklists. Winners will either receive a grant or be offered an investment from me to fund their idea with reasonable terms. I will start the contest annually and, as funds permit, I hope to eventually do the contest quarterly or maybe even monthly. I want to focus on helping fund good, well-planned businesses that might not otherwise get funding to start. Check the website for details on the Illegal To Legal Business Venture Competition.

I want to offer the funding because I believe the only way we can succeed and change our lives is if we help each other. Look at the immigrant groups that came to America. The most successful immigrants were the ones that did business with each other and helped each other out. We need to help each other succeed because the "system" isn't helping us do anything much more than to continue in crime or go back to prison.

Help me help you by spreading the word about this book. Mention it or buy it for your friends and family. Like us on our Facebook page "Illegal to Legal" and following us on Twitter. Please check the website for ongoing contest information, updates, and more free tools for you to use on your journey.

BUSINESS PLAN CHECKLIST™

What is a Business Plan Checklist™? I've developed it to be the bones and structure of a business plan without writing a long narrative. The purpose of it is to help you quickly identify and implement the tasks necessary for you to start and operate your business. If you are able, you should do a business plan. Whether you do a business plan or not, the Business Plan Checklist™ is a powerful tool to help you start planning and launch your business. Even if you don't fill it out completely it will help you immensely. Don't wait for perfect conditions before you start to work on the checklist.

There are a lot of questions to the Business Plan Checklist™. *Don't let the length of it bother you!* How do you eat an elephant? One bite at a time! The questions are for your benefit to help you be prepared for the success you want to achieve. Some questions will not apply to your situation so skip those items. You do not have to fill the Business Plan Checklist™ out in order. Fill out what you can as you get the answers figured out. It's OK to guess, just make it your best guess. After this is done, date it and put it in a separate file or notebook, one that you can refer to often.

As you launch out you will need to make some adjustments. That's normal and don't let that bother you. Continue to use the Business Plan Checklist™ tool and adjust as needed.

You do not have to have the Checklist done before you start your business. Use it as a tool to help you keep focused and moving forward. You might find it works better for you to complete it as you go. The important thing is for it to help you prepare, launch, operate, and grow your business.

There is a formatted easy to use Business Plan Checklist™ in Appendix A in Part 3 of this book, and also on the website illegaltolegal.org. Below is the text of the Business Plan Checklist™ with some explanations that don't occur on the form when you use it.

If you use the Business Plan Checklist™ as a guide to draft a business plan use common sense to tell the difference between items that you need to address in the Plan and items you simply do. Skip items that do not apply to your situation.

Enjoy the Business Plan Checklist™!

BUSINESS
-   What is the name of your business?

-   Have you Googled that name and checked with your Secretary of State to see if that name is available? You should register the business name with your Secretary of State and with a Domain registration service, as soon as you can so no one else uses it.

-   Why do you want to be in this business?

-   What is the need for this business?

-   Will you start this business from scratch, buy an existing business, or buy a franchise for this business?

-   What licensing, training, or experience do you need for this?

-   If you need licensing, training or experience for the business what is your plan to obtain them?

-   What is your work experience? Which jobs or tasks are relevant to this business?

- What is your experience in this business, if any?

- Do you need to work for a company in this field before starting your own business doing this or can you learn as you go?

- What do you believe your strengths in this business will be?

- Do you have a specialty or a niche you can serve?

- Who is your competition?

- Where are they located?

- What does your competition do well?

- What does your competition do poorly?

- What will make you unique or better than competition?

- What is your "elevator speech?" See the next chapter for an explanation and example.

- Have you made a map of your city which includes the location of your competition plus the location of any businesses that can be a positive or negative influence for you? See the Success Snapshot on a Martial Arts Studio for an example of how this can help you.

- Is the market underserved or saturated? Why do you think that?

- What is the target geographical area you will start serving? Expand to?

- What are the geographic limits of your service territory?

- What is your mission with your business, other than making money? (For most of my companies I usually use this as a mission statement: To make money by solving problems.)

- Do you have anyone you can get to mentor you in your new venture? (Preferably someone in the field or another successful businessperson that can take you under their wing). That is very important if you can get it.

- Who are your vendors and suppliers?

- What will you need to do to establish credit with them, and under what terms?

CUSTOMERS

- Who are your target customers? Why did you choose this group?

- How will you relate to or be relevant to this group? For instance, if you want a body shop that restores muscle cars, are you well known at the local muscle car shows?

- What is the estimated household income of your target customer? Is it above, below, or at the average household income for your target geographic area? What is their age? Household size? Do they own or rent? These items are called the demographics of your customers. If you don't know these things, you can get this information for free at the website of your local chamber of commerce or at census.gov. You can search for data by zip code or census tract. This is a very important step. For instance: if you want to start a daycare you wouldn't want to locate in a zip code without families with kids or that can't afford your services. If you want to start a home remodeling business targeting a specific area, make sure there are enough home owners there for you to make a living.

- How will you reach your customers? Door-to-door canvassing in a target area? This is called farming, and it's more effective than you think. I cover this in the Lawn Care Success Snapshot. You can use Google AdWords which is covered in the Snow Removal Success Snapshot and the Energy Auditor Success Snapshot.

- How will you advertise and promote your business?

- Will you, or how will you, use "social media?" (Facebook, You Tube, Twitter, LinkedIn, Craigslist, Amazon, EBay, email blasts, etc.)

- Do you know what the expected response rate of your proposed advertising is in your industry? Ask someone in your industry what worked for them or make the advertising representative give you references of existing customers that succeed with their product.

- What is your competition doing to advertise and promote?

- Will you offer a coupon, special, or other promotion? If so what?

PRODUCTS & SERVICES

- What is the cost and price of your product(s) or service(s)?

- How did you determine the cost and price?

- What is your starting inventory of product, if any?

- How does your product mix, inventory, and proposed prices compare with your competition?

- Do you need any licenses or permits to work in this area? Check with your city and state.

- Do you need to collect sales tax on your goods and services? Check with our state's Department of Revenue to confirm whether or not you need to collect sales tax, or pay use taxes. You may also need a state tax identification number as well which they can give you free.

- Do you need a logo? (We hope to eventually have a logo service available on our website).

- Do you need a website? There are several sites where you can do it for free yourself, like wix.com and weebly.com.

- Will you do sales over the internet? If so I recommend Paypal as a payment processing option. GoDaddy has built-in e-commerce capability available as well.

- Who will do your order fulfillment?

ADMINISTRATIVE, STAFFING, OWNERSHIP

- When can you get business cards? Overnightprints.com, Vista Print, and Office Depot offer affordable starter packages. If you want to develop local business relationships nearly any local printer can give you a competitive printing package as well. You can also print your own business cards on your computer if you wish.

- Where will you do your banking at? I recommend trying to find a local business-oriented bank where you have or can establish relationship. Having a business banker that knows you is a critical key to succeeding long term. Also when you bank, don't move your personal account where your business accounts are. The temptation to "rob Peter to pay Paul" might be too great if you keep the accounts at the same bank. God knows you don't want to repeat the same mistake that got me my time!

- Do you need to accept credit cards? Square is a great smart-phone based credit card reader/payment system, and there are numerous credit cards services to choose from.

- How many employees do you need? How much will you pay them?

- What are the job positions, and how many of each, do you need to fill to function? Sales, production, accounting, support, labor, etc.?

- How do you intend to run it, or how do you think it will run? Is it just you, or will you hire managers? Do you have family members to help out?

- How will you train them and supervise them?

- Will you use subcontractors?

- Can you operate your business from home or do you need to rent a shop, store, or office space?

- How much space do you need for your business?

- Do you have a good commercial real estate agent to help you? Instead of buying real estate first I always recommend to lease with an option to purchase, and let the future profits from your business pay for the real estate.

- Do you need to maintain a service department? If so, what do you need for facilities, equipment, staff, and supplies to operate it?

- What are you doing to provide customer service?

- How will it be owned? Will you own it yourself, or incorporate, or make an LLC (limited liability company) or a partnership? You don't have to incorporate to start, but you should have a separate checking account for the business whether or not you incorporate.

- Who are the owners of the business? List percentages of ownership and the responsibilities of all owners or partners.

- If it is a corporation, who are the officers?

- What is the "chain of command?"

FURNITURE, FIXTURES, AND EQUIPMENT (FF & E)

- What equipment, tools, computers, vehicles, and furniture do you need to have?

- Where can you buy them? Can you buy them used for less than new?

- What will each item cost? Is there a monthly payment associated with them?

- How will you pay for them? A loan? Personal funds? Money from a partner or investor? Will you lease or rent them? Can you get these items on a payment plan, or with delayed payment, and pay for them from the operation of your new business?

INSURANCE and LEGAL

- How much will your insurance cost? You will be surprised how affordable business insurance is. If you are short of funds, have insurance, and incorporate later. Customers have more comfort with your proof of insurance, which will help you get more business.

- Do you have an attorney? You don't need one to start, but should think about finding one as your business grows.

FINANCIAL

- Do you have an Employer ID Number (also known as a Tax ID number?) You can get these free at irs.gov. They have links for doing business in each state. Follow those links to get free state tax ID #s also.

- Do you have a Certified Public Accountant (CPA) or bookkeeper?

- Who will maintain your records? Who will handle your finances?

- What are your start-up costs? This is included in the Business Plan Checklist™ in Appendix A and on the website for your free use.

- How much of the start-up costs do you have now?

- What can you do to raise money, if needed? Do you have friends, family, a bank, or an investor you can approach? For any money that you invest in your business personally you should book that as a loan to the business to minimize the taxes you pay on business earnings. For it to be valid in the eyes of the IRS you must actually sign a promissory note from the business to yourself, with an interest rate.

- How much money will you need to operate at each stage? Meaning, what is your overhead? If you have to guess then guess on the high side of things instead of the low side. Try to be as realistic as you can, and take into account all elements of the business such as: payroll, rent, utilities, insurance, vehicle expense, payroll taxes, income taxes, debt service, supplies, materials, repairs, travel, marketing, collection loss, legal/professional fees, etc. Add any items that are missing.

- What is your overhead, monthly and annually?

- How much money will you need to operate for the first three months? Six months? Year? Two years?

- Make a monthly budget showing your projected income and expenses for the next two years.

- How did you determine the future income?

- Given all of these factors and costs, what is your best guess as to how long it is before it is profitable? This is called your "break-even point." I believe delays in being profitable can be minimized with proper planning and execution of your plan. Having extra cash on hand, or access to it or another source of income, is never a bad thing either.

- How long does it take you to get to your break-even point? If there is a projected cash shortfall, how do you intend to deal with it?

- When will you open your checking accounts? Always have a business checking account, and a personal account, and never mix the two funds as doing so makes your bookkeeping complicated and could trigger an audit or worse. I'm speaking from personal experience here! When you want to use money from your business simply note the transfer or use of funds form the business to yourself.

What do you do if your credit is so bad that you cannot open a bank account? Do what I did – get a Walmart Prepaid Debit Card. It's free if you deposit a minimal monthly amount. With it you can then open a free PayPal account, and get a PayPal business debit card. Between those two options, and cashing checks at the banks they were written at, you should be able to have an account to start.

CHAPTER 6

UNCONVENTIONAL THINGS TO KNOW BEFORE YOU START

I hope and pray you are finding this book useful. I've tried to be very practical and give you information and strategies to help you get into your own business as quickly as possible. This chapter is devoted to giving you important things to keep in mind as you get ready to launch your business. I have unconventional opinions about most of these items. Whether you agree with me or not I hope I get you to think about what your position is on these topics. Each of these items could be a book in itself, so these elements are only introductions to these areas. Check the website for free downloads of booklets on these topics, more of which will be added over time.

Dr. John C. Maxwell tells the story of an exuberant young person who insistently asked him "What is the <u>one thing</u> I need to know to be a good leader?" John answered by saying "the one thing you need to know to be a good leader is that there is more than one thing you need to know to be a good leader!"

I think there are two basic things you need to know as you start a successful business. By no means is that all you need to know but they are a strong beginning of your journey to survive and thrive. These two things are:

1. A Unique Selling Proposition (USP), also known as a "purple cow."
2. A good Elevator Speech.

The other things in this chapter are very helpful also, but you absolutely have to have a mastery of these first two things or I believe your journey will be more difficult than it needs to be.

UNIQUE SELLING PROPOSITION (USP) – the "Purple Cow"

Seth Godin wrote an amazing little marketing and business book you should read called *The Purple Cow*. The book is about how to market and run your business in a way to find and promote your unique selling proposition - your "purple cow." The concept of a purple cow is this: pretend you've never been to the country before, and you see a cow for the first time. Naturally you get excited. But after your 500th cow, it's no big deal. But if you saw a purple cow, you would remember that cow and tell everyone you knew about that unique experience!

So what makes your business unique? What do you do or offer that your competition doesn't? What can you do to distinguish yourself as a unique business, a purple cow, as opposed to another studio in a strip mall? Do you have a unique selling proposition or are you the 501st cow?

If there are 100 lawn services in your market, why should they pick you? I hope it's not just because you're the cheapest. Being cheap is a good way to start, but you must quickly learn to build a loyal customer base in order to grow. What do you do better, or differently, than anyone else? Are you the most prompt? Do you have the best customer service? Maybe you email the customer after each mow to make sure they are satisfied.

To survive in a competitive environment you have to have something that people remember you by, so they remember to buy.

MARKETING, SALES, & THE ELEVATOR SPEECH

Marketing and Sales will make or break your business. A lot of people say "sales and marketing" but without the proper marketing there will be no sales. To me, marketing is the process of telling your story and why customers should use your business. Selling is using the marketing tools to make the sale. All the marketing in the world won't help you if you cannot make the sale.

The late Senator Tip O'Neill once said "all politics is local." I say "all marketing is personal." Farming, or targeting a specific geographic area, is a tried and true method to build a business. I like the right internet marketing, such as Google AdWords, but I don't think anything beats personal marketing and a good elevator speech.

An elevator speech (also known as an elevator pitch) is a quick and memorable way to tell your story in a way that should introduce and promote your business and help you make more sales. It's called an "elevator speech" because it's designed to be said quickly within the same two minutes or so that it takes you to ride an elevator.

What do you use an elevator speech for? Try this experiment: make note of how many times a day you are asked what you do for a living. Your elevator speech is your answer, and your best chance to create a new customer. People have a short attention span, and if it's too long they will lose interest and you will lose a sale.

> *"All marketing is personal."*
> *-Pelshaw's Principles of Profitable Business*

CUSTOMER SERVICE

Customer Service is one of the best ways to make your purple cow. Always go the extra mile. Is the customer always right? No. Some customers will try to take advantage of you. Even so, treat everyone with respect, focus your customer service, and operate in a way that makes it easy for people to do business with you, and refer business to you.

No matter how you operate your business there will always be problems that arise. No one is perfect. What makes great customer service and a great company is how you deal with situations and complaints that happen. Handle your customers and their complaints with the Golden Rule: Treat others as you want to be treated. Then you will turn your customer service into a purple cow.

PRICING

Pricing is one of the hardest things to get right. Check what your competition is doing for prices, and don't be afraid to charge more. Just make sure you are worth it.

I have a friend that built a successful concrete laying business specializing in driveways. He has built a reputation of quoting all jobs within 48 hours of a customer inquiry and for being on the job when he promised to be there. He charges more than his competition. In response to a $5,000 bid a customer may tell my friend "Your competition bid this for $4,000 aren't you going to match that price?" He'll respond by saying *"Where is the competition? If they were going to honor that bid why am I here ready to give you a guaranteed start and completion date?"* He usually gets the job.

The hardest part about pricing is knowing the full extent of everything you need to include to accurately know what to charge. In the old days you could take the cost of material and double it to get a ballpark range of what to charge a customer. To accurately price your goods or services you need to include a cost for all of your overhead, reserves, employees, and taxes. A good CPA or bookkeeper can help you with this.

SPECIAL LICENSING OR TRAINING

Some of these businesses require you to have a special license, equipment, tools, vehicle(s), computer(s), or training. Check on the internet to find the rules and regulations governing your new business, and incorporate the results into your Business Plan Checklist ™.

INCOME REPORTING & TAXES

You may think I'm crazy, but I think paying taxes is a good thing. I like paying taxes. Paying taxes means I'm making money. Basically I love to create income tax problems by earning a lot of money! If you're making money you have something to show a bank when you need to borrow. Making money creates value for your business if you ever decide to sell it. I don't want to overpay taxes, and I am aggressive about taking whatever write-offs I can. Set aside 15 percent of the gross income of your business off the top so you always have the cash to pay your taxes. Your tax bill should be less than that, so any excess money you have you can use to reinvest in your business or keep building up your capital. Remember that the Internal Revenue Service (IRS) has made felons out of many people who didn't pay their taxes!

BACKGROUND CHECKS & BONDING

Some licensing and training require background checks. Don't let this stop you from pursuing your dream. Just because they may perform a background check doesn't mean you'll fail, especially if some time has passed since you broke the law (if you have a criminal record, that is). There is a free bonding program for felons. For more information look at bonds4jobs.com/. Having a bond, either from this site or from your insurance agent should get you past any negative background checks.

I recommend having a short statement prepared to explain any negative information they will find. Submit it along with the background check request. Letting them know up front shows character. In your letter you will explain and show examples of how you've changed. You'll also let them know how badly you want to pass the background check so you can get started in your new venture. The fact that you may be a felon actually could be spun to their advantage, as most felons in their right minds don't want to violate their probation or get another charge. Therefore there is extra assurance that you will likely perform better than someone who has yet to offend.

BUYING TOOLS AND EQUIPMENT

Try to have as much tools and equipment as you can reasonably afford, but don't go overboard. I recommend you get the minimum needed to start, and then let the cash flow from your new business pay for more tools and equipment. If having more tools and equipment up front gets you more business, then by all means buy as much as you can reasonably afford and still maintain as big a financial cushion as possible. Remember it's more important to get the business started than to have every gadget and gizmo up front. Don't be "tool rich" and "cash poor!"

Check Craigslist, pawn shops, garage sales, self-storage auctions, police auctions, and estate sales for deals on tools, equipment, and vehicles. Many stores will sell the floor model or have a section where they sell returned items for drastic discounts. Don't be afraid to ask your family and friends to be on the lookout for things for you as well.

SHOULD I INCORPORATE?

You don't have to be incorporated before you start your business. Conventional wisdom says you need to be incorporated for liability protection. I say you can always incorporate later after you have established the business. It is far better to spend the money on insurance to begin with, and incorporate when you can afford it. Business insurance is cheaper than you think, and many customers won't work with a business that isn't insured for at least liability coverage.

SEPARATE CHECKING ACCOUNT

You should have a separate checking account for your new business, even if you don't incorporate it. This is very important when it comes time to paying your taxes and organizing your finances. Don't use your company as a personal piggy bank. That's what got me in trouble, even though it was all my own money. If you want to pull money out, pay it to yourself as salary or an owner draw and then spend your money. Even if you don't have partners, don't comingle personal funds with company funds. Your life will be easier and better that way. _Do_ keep and mark all of your receipts and maximize the expenses you can write off.

EMPLOYEES

Other than having enough capital, I think employees are the biggest issue facing growing businesses. Don't be afraid to hire employees that may be better than you. The wildly successful ad executive David Ogilvy tells the story of how his company was facing challenges and was at a crossroads where they would either explode in growth or not survive. He brought his directors together and gave them all a box. Inside the box was a Russian doll. Russian dolls start with an outer doll, which you open to reveal another smaller doll, and so forth. Inside the last doll was this message: "If we continue to hire … people [with lesser abilities] than ourselves we will quickly become a company of dwarves."

Failing to train your workforce or delegate more tasks to them makes them dwarves also. When you raise the water level all the ships rise. Grow your company by growing your people. Regularly read self-help books and magazines. Study leadership, and read books from John Maxwell, Andy Stanley, John Wooden, and Zig Ziglar. Get your staff to read and listen to material as well. Go to the annual Leadercast webinar held every May leadercast.com. Attend conferences to strengthen your strengths and help the weaknesses that weakens you and your team.

> *"If we continue to hire...people [with lesser abilities] than ourselves we will quickly become a company of dwarves."*
>
> *-David Ogilvy*

PARTNERS
A partnership is truly like a marriage: you are stuck with each other and must work to make your partnership work. The best partnerships are ones where the partners have strengths and weaknesses that complement each other, and they meaningfully and equally contribute to each other and the partnership. Don't be partners with someone unless you trust them with your life, because that is what they have in their hands.

MONEY MANAGEMENT
I love what John Wesley says about finances: Earn all you can. Save all you can. Give all you can. Dave Ramsey has a nationally syndicated radio show that gives entertaining advice about money management. Common sense tells us to live within our means and save as much money as possible. We can say that, but I can tell you from personal experience doing it is another story.

The best advice I have on saving money is to treat your savings account like a bill that you must pay every month. Robert Kiyosaki, author of *Rich Dad, Poor Dad* says to pay yourself first.

INVESTING

Investing is the highest form of business. Investing is when you have extra resources you want to put to work that don't require your day-to-day involvement. I have eight principles below that I follow for investing, (These are also included at the end of *Appendix D*: Pelshaw's Principles for Profitable Business).

1. I never invest in anything I don't understand.
2. I never invest in anything I don't control unless I trust the other parties so much that I don't have to control it.
3. The return *of* money is more important than return *on* money.
4. Create cash flow by solving problems, and invest the cash flow to create more wealth.
5. Know your strengths and weaknesses, and always focus on your strengths.
6. I try to achieve a five-year payback minimum for any investment unless it is a very safe conservative investment.
7. Make money by exploiting opportunities created by solving problems.
8. Make your money on the "Buy" by buying something for the best price possible.

SHOULD I RENT AN OFFICE OR SHOP, OR IS IT BETTER TO WORK FROM HOME?

I don't believe you need an office or shop to start as long as you have a place you can function until you can afford to grow into your own space. Rule #1 to Pelshaw's Principles for Profitable Business is "everything must pay for itself." Hopefully you grow fast enough to enable you to afford whatever you need and desire. I have worked from an office and from home. Each offers advantages and disadvantages.

> *"Everything has to pay for itself."*
> *-Pelshaw's Principles of Profitable Business*

Working from home saves money and commuting time, but there is a tendency to work all of the time instead of leaving your work at the office. If you have kids, working from home is a great way to share life with them and maybe save on childcare. So many people work from home now that there really isn't a negative stigma associated with home based businesses anymore.

Your local zoning or laws may prevent you from working from home, but if not, working from home is a great way to start. Who knows, you may like it so much you might never go back.

Before you rent an office or shop, look for a place that will share their space with you or sublet part of their space to you. As your business grows, you can then move into a bigger place.

ACCOUNTING & BOOKKEEPING

Your business is a lot like a tree: it can only grow as far as the roots can support. The "roots" in your business are your paperwork, accounting, and bookkeeping systems.

To start your business, work on a "Cash Basis." That is an accounting term that is exactly what it sounds like: your bookkeeping in based on recording your cash flows in and out. With the cash basis your bookkeeping basically works just like balancing a check book. Use Quicken or QuickBooks for an accounting software package. Those are easy to learn, and there are many bookkeeping professionals that can set up and do your books for you reasonably if you aren't able to tackle it yourself.

Keeping up on your books is critically important, especially if you ever want to get a bank loan, buy a large item for the business, want to see what you're really making, or ever want to sell the company. The more income you can document, the more your company, and ultimately you, are worth, and the more you can borrow if needed. Without the proper record keeping you're just another unorganized, unprofessional schmuck instead of a talented, organized, credible business person. **Do your paperwork and records regularly! Many great businesses have failed because they fell behind on their paperwork.**

My friend Craig has a successful subcontracting business. He says a key to his success is his standing appointment to sit and work with his bookkeeper every Friday morning from 8 AM to 10 AM. Joyce Meyers says, "Getting organized in the normal routines of life and finishing little projects you've started is an important first step toward realizing larger goals. If you can't get a handle on the small things, how will you ever get it together to focus on the big things?"

PAPERWORK AND RECEIPTS

Whenever you get a receipt *immediately* write in ink, legibly, on the receipt what the receipt is for (what expense category it fits in). Once you're in the habit of this, it shouldn't take you more than 20 or 30 seconds to do it. Trying to do it at the end of the year, when you're stressed about filing taxes, will take you a lot more time.

> *"Do your paperwork and records regularly! Many great businesses have failed because they fell behind on their paperwork."*
>
> -R.L. Pelshaw

A friend of mine who owns a successful lawn business has three bank bags in each of his trucks. One bag is for the carbon copies of the work statements his crew leaves with each customer. One bag is for receipts if the customer pays for services. The last bag is for expenses. I keep a folder for receipts and a folder for bills. Whichever way you choose, find something that works for you and do it consistently.

Here's a powerful tool to help you handle your paperwork and books. I have a rule about paper and receipts. I try to touch them as few of times as possible, because many people waste a lot of time moving paper around. For every paper I get I either:

1. Act on it.
2. Delegate it.
3. File it.
4. Throw it away.

Most businesses generate a receipt or invoice when work is completed. If you do this on your computer, make sure you do them in duplicate. If you do them by hand, you can buy carbon paper and fill them out in duplicate, giving your customer the original and keeping a copy for yourself. These invoices/receipts are a great way to help you keep track of your gross earnings, which is how much you earn before your expenses.

You can also take the customer information from your invoices and make your own database of customers. If they are satisfied, they would love to get occasional coupons and specials emailed to them. Giving loyal customers discounts is a cheap form of advertising and driving repeat business. Reward them for referring new customers.

Stay in the habit of marking your receipts, invoices, and statements **DAILY**. If you do it daily it should only take a few minutes each day. You brush your teeth daily, you bathe or shower regularly: keeping up with your receipts is the business equivalent of brushing your teeth or showering. You have to do it regularly or things really stink.

If you don't mark them daily, then make a set appointment on our calendar every week to input your receipts, whether you do your books or someone else does. DO NOT procrastinate and let the receipts pile up until you have a big pile. Daily input is best, but at least do it weekly.

FREE RESOURCES

There are free resources available to you to help you start your business and guide you along the way. For instance, the Small Business Administration, S.C.O.R.E., Business Incubators, Business Development Centers, Colleges, Universities, and many chambers of commerce have programs and people who give free advice.

Some local chambers of commerce have networking events and "Tip Clubs" that are regular meetings of business professionals to help give each other leads and referrals. These are a few of the great ways to let other businesses know about your new venture.

A good website to look at if you are interested in acquiring an existing business or franchise is bizbuysell.com/. Even if you don't buy a business that's listed there, you learn about what businesses for sale are worth, and use that to your advantage. For instance, let's say you found a local hair salon you want to buy, and you don't know if the asking price for the business is too high. You can look at the sales price of other hair salons and see if yours is priced right or not. If it's too high you can always tell the seller you found other salons listed for "x" price and then tell that seller what you would be willing to pay. Some time on the internet finding comparable or similar businesses for sale just saved you thousands of dollars.

LoopNet, a part of the CoStar Group, is a leading free commercial real estate listing service where you can find available properties for sale or lease, as well as vital market and demographic information. You will learn more about LoopNet in the Martial Arts Studio Success Snapshot and at loopnet.com. Check out daveramsey.com for the best free resources on money management, budgeting, paying off debt quickly, investing, and more.

The website for Dr. John C. Maxwell johnmaxwell.com has several free subscription resources available including *A Minute With Maxwell* and *John Maxwell Presents*. They are very meaningful and well worth your time.

My website illegaltolegal.org has additional resources we will continue to add to, most of which are free.

THINGS TO READ TO HELP YOU START:
This final section is devoted to recommended reading. We include an updated version of this on the website illegaltolegal.org. Most of these books below are available as books on CD if it's easier for you to listen to a book than read it. If you cannot afford to buy them you can of course check them out from your local public library.

Please let us know if there are other books you recommend on the reading list to help (ex) criminals launch into legitimate business.

RICH DAD, POOR DAD by Robert Kiyosaki
THE RICHEST MAN IN BABYLON by George Samuel Clason
TOTAL MONEY MAKEOVER - Dave Ramsey
FINANCIAL PEACE UNIVERSITY - Dave Ramsey
FAILING FORWARD – John C. Maxwell
TODAY MATTERS - John C. Maxwell
THINKING FOR A CHANGE - John C. Maxwell
THE 21 IRREFUTABLE LAWS OF LEADERSHIP - John C. Maxwell
THE PURPLE COW - Seth Godin
THE TRAVELER'S GIFT – Andy Andrews
STRENGTHSFINDERS 2.0 – Tom Rath
SUCCESS MAGAZINE
ZIGLAR ON SELLING – Zig Ziglar
REACHING THE TOP – Zig Ziglar

Part Two

SUCCESS SNAPSHOTS
OF ACTUAL BUSINESSES

SUCCESS SNAPSHOTS
OF ACTUAL BUSINESSES

So far we've covered the fact that you are entrepreneurial, have strengths, passions, picked out some potential businesses to start, and even reviewed important items for you to know and implement as you start your new venture.

It wouldn't be fair to get you excited about starting a business without giving you some practical examples, with more detail, to help you actually start your business. This section of the book has examples from some of the businesses to start as listed in Chapter 4. Each example includes actual testimonials from people who have started their business from scratch and built it into something successful. I call their stories "Success Snapshots." Any financial returns or facts they reported were not verified and are provided for inspirational and conversational purposes only. Several of the business owners interviewed opted to remain confidential so I used an assumed name to protect their identities. When I do this I include the assumed name in quotes, like "Ben" or "Barry." You will be encouraged and motivated by their stories which they shared to help inspire you on your journey.

If this were a textbook I would give you a definition for every item I wanted to introduce you to. Instead I use the real life stories in the Success Snapshots to teach you important lessons about legitimate business. I hope you find this format exciting, meaningful, and especially practical.

When coupled with your Street University degree each Success Snapshot will not only let you know about a particular business, but will also demonstrate a vital skill you will need to successfully launch and operate your new business. By reading all of the Success Snapshots you might even find the business you should start or ones you shouldn't.

I tried to select people with typical obstacles and occurrences, but your own story will differ from theirs. Their path is but one way to succeed. You may find a better way. Let their story inspire you to start your own business and eventually be able to create your own personal Success Snapshot. Share your story on our website, perhaps you will be featured online, or in the next book.

The website illlegaltolegal.org has these examples, the Business Plan Checklist™, actual business plans, and more for your free use. As you know, if you need greater help, a customized Business Plan Checklist™, business plan, a logo, or even business coaching are available as well.

The Success Snapshot examples may or may not be representative of what you could achieve if you started the same businesses. They are by no means guarantees of anything other than inspiration and knowledge. There are a lot of factors that will affect how quickly or slowly your business succeeds, if it succeeds at all. It is mostly dependent on you. Will you make the sacrifices to prepare, plan, organize, promote, manage, and grow your business? For the most part, how well you succeed is totally dependent on how dedicated you are to making it succeed. If you stay in the process long enough for it to happen. It won't be easy, but it will be one of the most rewarding things you've ever accomplished if you stick with it and work hard and smart enough.

For every example, where I give you an estimate of the cash required to start the business, I assume:

1. You have a decent running vehicle, if possible.
2. You have a computer with whatever software you need.
3. You have a smartphone that can text and email.
4. Your living expenses are covered.

I intentionally do not include "working capital" or "cash reserves" into the estimate of your start-up funds. You may not have any cash reserves. Don't let a lack of cash keep you from your dream. In a perfect world you would have six months of business operating expense and living expense. However, don't let a lack of funds stop you from starting a business: build up the cash as you go; just be very careful with your spending.

With every business if you have a chance to go to work for someone in that field already, do that to get experience and save some money as you can. You may find after doing the work that you like something else better, so it's always a good idea to first work for someone else while you try something out, learn, and save up money.

Regardless of what business you decide to start, check with your state and city to see if any licenses or permits are required.

Finally, the income and expense estimates are for discussion purposes only, they are not guaranteed, and will vary widely based on your market, competition, pricing, and the effort you put in your business.

With all of that, is it still worth trying to start your own business? _Absolutely_!

I hope you realize you, your future, and the future of your family are worth you busting through, beating the odds, and making a business you can be proud of.

I'm here to cheer you on. I believe in you!!

SUCCESS SNAPSHOT

TRUCKING

What Is Your "Waterpark Moment?"

"Know Your Potential - It Will Help You Make Better Decisions"

INCOME: $75,000 - $150,000/year or more.

LICENSING and TRAINING: a Class "A" Commercial Driver's License (CDL) is required. Some states require classroom time or formal training to earn a CDL. Other states simply want you to pass a written test, vision test, and a driving test. Check with your state's Department of Motor Vehicles to learn what is required where you live. Many trucking companies will offer to pay for your schooling and CDL with a commitment to work for them.

SPECIAL SKILLS: must love driving, be very dependable, and be a self-starter. Before books on CD, Kindle, Ipods, and Ipads it used to be that a trucker needed to love spending time alone, but with technology, you can use your windshield time for self-improvement.

EXPERIENCE: none other than driving.

START-UP COSTS:
Anywhere from $0 to $5,000 if you want to be a trucker for someone else or a sole owner operator who leases a vehicle. You can buy an old used truck for as little as $10,000, but let the buyer beware: you get what you pay for. It may be good enough to get you started in the business. Then reinvest your profits into a better truck when you can afford it. You will need from $30,000 to $70,000 minimum if you want to start your own trucking firm or operate multiple trucks.

NEED TO INCORPORATE: It is not necessary to incorporate to initially start truck driving, but to be a trucking company you should incorporate as an "S" Corporation or a Limited Liability Company (LLC). Your tax advisor can help you decide which is best for you. Don't pay more than a few hundred dollars to incorporate. Incorporation papers are available at our website for you to form your own do-it-yourself LLC for a fraction of what an attorney would charge. Or course, we are not giving legal advice to you, just helping you save money by doing it yourself.

Before writing this Success Snapshot I didn't know how profitable trucking could be. Everything made, produced, grown, mined, bought, assembled, or getting ready to be sold has to be shipped someplace. There are a lot of ways to make money as a trucker, from being an employee, being a single truck owner-operator, to owning your own trucking company with drivers working for you. You can haul locally, and be home with your family every evening, or you can drive coast to coast. You can haul gravel, grain, or go-carts. There's such a thing as being a "hot shot hauler" which means you transport loads on an emergency basis on short notice, and make a lot of money doing it.

How much money can you earn? Over $100,000 per year is easily attainable, and that's if you only drive one truck. Start to own multiple trucks, with drivers working for you, and that number increases quickly. Your earnings depend on you, your market, what you are hauling, and whether you are driving locally or over a distance. Plus, your income will be different owning your own truck versus driving someone else's. Check out Ike's story below. Ike was able to make something from nothing and turn it into his own successful three-truck company.

IKE'S STORY:
Ike grew up in the projects where gang activity was rampant in the large Midwestern city he called home. Although he and his friends had a lot of influence there, he always felt like he was destined for more. He wanted to help people achieve a better life.

He later worked his way into a community college. Like most new college students he partied a great deal. He told me he often would lie to himself by saying "I'll go out tonight and wake up early to study." Ike was sacrificing the ultimate (his education, his future) on the altar of the immediate (partying and having fun instead of studying). Ike's story isn't pretty at this point: he flunked out of school as he didn't have good study skills.

"Don't sacrifice the ultimate on the altar of the immediate."

Soon Ike straightened up, stopped lying to himself, and returned to classes. He took school seriously, like it was his job, and he earned all As and Bs. He thought he could help his people most by studying criminal justice. After earning an associate's degree he transferred to a university to earn a bachelor's degree.

Just before graduation he realized a career in criminal justice wasn't what he really wanted to do. Instead, Ike started studying accounting and eventually got his degree and a job in that field.

By chance, hanging out at a water park, Ike bumped into an old friend. He asked his friend what he was up to, and when his friend told him he was making $75/hour driving a truck locally, Ike got excited! That was a lot more money than he was making doing accounting, and he could be his own boss.

This was Ike's "waterpark moment:" the moment when you are presented with a vision for a new future, a new destiny, a new challenge that excites you and uses your passions and strengths. Perhaps reading this book is your "waterpark moment." Ike seized the moment and asked his friend permission to go along with him, for free, during the day to observe his work. His friend hauled asphalt locally.

After a few months of observing and learning the business from his friend, (and asking every question he could think of) Ike got his CDL. His friend helped him get into his first truck in January 2006. Ike, with his friend's help and guidance, built that one truck into a three-truck trucking company. Since Ike has more than one truck, Ike tries to pay forward the help he received by only hiring people who could benefit from using trucking to get out of poverty and gangs. Ike is living out his dream of helping his people.

There's a Chinese proverb that says "when the student is ready the teacher will appear." Without knowing that proverb, Ike proved it to be true through the relationship he had with his friend from the waterpark. His friend became his teacher and mentor when Ike took the initiative to learn trucking from him. Now Ike is mentoring others.

Everyone should have a mentor, if possible. The right mentor can make the difference between success and failure. Everyone, when able, should also be a mentor. You will find it makes you a better businessman, and a better person. We reap what we sow, so why not sow good things into others?

Here are some tips from me on selecting a mentor, and on selecting people to mentor:

1.   Select a mentor that is solid, keeps his word, is credible and skilled, and wants to help you.

2.   Be open to the possibility that their mentoring may only be a one-time conversation, or it may be ongoing.

3.   Be careful when you select someone to mentor. Look for potential, work ethic, and reliability. Dr. John C. Maxwell tells this story about a man that he spoke with during a break at a conference featuring Maxwell. The man factored the admission price multiplied by the number of people attending and saw big profits. He went to Maxwell, told him what he calculated, and then said "I want to do what you do for a living." When you are successful, many people will come to you and say they want to do what you do or earn what you earn and ask you for help. So how do you tell which ones to help and which ones not to? Maxwell answered the man's statement by saying "*you may want to do what I do, but you don't want to do <u>what I did</u> so I can do what I do.*"

When approached to help someone, look for that person who is willing to pay the price, not just make more money. Keep in mind that just because you want them to do better, doesn't mean *they* want to do better. You cannot give them inner-drive or hustle. Either they have it or they don't. Look for and hire people that have their own inner-drive, and are not looking for you to do it for them.

4.   If you want to attract a mentor, be that person with inner-drive yourself. Have written questions thought out and prepared in advance of when you meet with your mentor. Take notes when they answer your questions. Thank them for their help, and let them be part of your success journey.

Here are some suggestions from Ike on the keys to success in the trucking business:

1.   Work for someone as a driver first, so you can learn the ins and outs of the business.

2.   Once licensed, you can get into a new truck for about $5,000 down, but you will be heavily in debt and have a big payment to make. Do not put yourself into debt until you can secure steady long-term contracts to cover your monthly payment.

3. Instead of going into debt for a truck, sacrifice for two to three years, saving all the money you can and building up your credit, so you can buy your own truck and launch when you are ready without the big monthly payment or debt.

4. You can get work through trucking and shipping brokers who usually take a 10 percent charge based on the work they send you.

5. Regularly visit job sites and companies that use the type of trucking you will perform. Let them know you are available for shipping if they need it. While there, find out who arranges for shipping in the company. By "regularly" I mean make it your daily habit. In business lingo this is called "cold calling." On the streets, you called it "hustling." It's the same thing.

6. Anyone shipping with a truck is a good lead to pursue for extra work. Let all of them know you do trucking and are available to help them sometimes. Leave a card, and get a card from them if you can. Stay organized and keep track of who you visit by keeping a notebook or spreadsheet of the contact. From there you can make an email list and send them a little newsletter or occasional email. At the very least after you meet them you should email them or send them a note or a phone call within three days of your visit to remember you by. Something like "I enjoyed meeting you yesterday to discuss your trucking needs. Please let me know when I can be of service. I'm looking forward to serving you soon." Afterwards, check in with them once a month or so. Do you want to really impress them? Find out when your contact's birthday is, and send him a card or an email. Build a relationship. Who knows what may come of it? Soon you will have so much work you'll have to start buying trucks and hiring drivers like Ike did.

7. Be adaptable. Without it, Ike would've never left his accounting job for his own trucking business. Besides, you never know when God will bring you to your own "waterpark moment," which is when you are presented the opportunity for a different future. But _you_ have to take the initiative. Ike's friend didn't offer to help set him up in a trucking business. Ike had to express interest and investigate and pursue driving for himself. His friend helped after Ike showed interest.

8. Speaking of being adaptable, when it rained Ike didn't work hauling gravel, so he arranged to haul scrap metal on rainy days. This ensured his income wouldn't be dependent on the weather.

9. Be responsible. All you have is your reputation and your word. You will build your business, or kill it, based on how well you keep your word.

10. When you get a new customer or a new trucking broker, be prepared to wait as it could be a couple of months before your first paycheck comes in. That is why good cash reserves or a bank line of credit are important to have as soon as you can.

11. You get what you pay for when it comes to trucks. Know the type of hauling you are going to do, and get the best vehicle suited for that hauling that you can afford.

Some final thoughts from Ike:

To be successful, accept no excuses from yourself. Make the sacrifices and stay committed until you reach the success you know you can achieve.

Do you know why LeBron James, when he was graduating high school, didn't take a job at McDonald's? It was because he knew who he was, and what his potential was. ***You have great potential***: potential far beyond whatever you could make illegally.

Don't sacrifice the ultimate on the altar of the immediate. You can go make a lot of money doing something illegal but you will sacrifice the ultimate (your future) for the immediate cash. **DON'T DO IT** - take the slower, safer route. It will make you more money in the long run and you will stay out of jail.

> *"When you know your potential, you tend to do better and you make better decisions."*
>
> *-Ike*

Don't just read this book and do nothing afterwards. Maybe this book is your "waterpark moment."

SUCCESS SNAPSHOT

MARTIAL ARTS STUDIO

ALSO APPLIES TO A: BOXING GYM, DANCE STUDIO, FITNESS STUDIO, YOGA STUDIO, ETC.

*"It's OK To Fall Down - You Have To Learn
To Fall Right To Fight"*

I use this Success Story to give a real-life demonstration of:

- How to use demographic data to identify your target customer.
- How to select a target market.
- How to do site selection for retail and service businesses.
- How to research the competition, and do market research.

These items apply to any retail store, service business, restaurant, or other businesses that rely on walk-in customer traffic. Please read this section to learn more.

INCOME RANGE: $5,000 - $15,000/month or more.

START-UP COSTS: Less than $1,000 if you rent a school gym, church hall, community center, or other "pay as you go" venue, then build business up until you can afford to rent someplace permanent. If you lease space you can open for $10,000 provided you have minimal payroll expense.

TRAINING OR SKILLS REQUIRED: Patience. Also, be a "people person" as all you have to sell is yourself; be in good physical condition and have the experience and personality to train in martial arts and self-defense

LICENSING REQUIRED: No

NEED TO INCORPORATE: Recommended.

From young to old, millions are flocking to martial arts for fun, exercise, and to learn self-defense and positive life skills. The popularity of Mixed

Martial Arts and Ultimate Fighting television shows and events have helped fuel more excitement for this sport.

Location, location, location (with a side of demographics)
A great location is the key to the success of a new martial arts studio or any business that depends on customer traffic. How do you select a "great location?" Be strategic and start with the end in mind by identifying your customer you wish to serve, where they are coming from, and the market where you want to serve them. Let those factors lead you to the proper neighborhood and location. For instance:

1. If you want to work with kids find neighborhoods with young families. Rank them by household income, family size, and how close a competing martial arts studio is. Being near a military base or a shopping center is a major help to attract business from families.

2. If you want to work with females, locate near a Target, Walmart, Crafts Store (like Hobby Lobby or Michael's), or a popular hair salon. Always note how close the nearest competition is.

3. Do you want to target fitness customers? Locate near popular health clubs, sports fields, or popular health supplement stores in areas where the household income and age matches the type of customer you want.

4. If you want to work with military clientele locate near the military base and advertise where military personnel and contractors will notice you.

5. If you want to work with the mixed martial arts crowd sponsor MMA events or advertise at them. Make your ads target the customers you want to attract.

6. Try to get the highest profile location you can on the busiest street with the best access. Make sure you are on the side of the street that matches your business. If you are a coffee shop you want to be on the "going to" side of the street to catch people going to work. If you are a burger joint you might want to be on the "going home" side of the street. Try to avoid a one-way street unless you are sure it's a great location.

7.   Check with your local city planning or traffic departments to find the traffic counts for your location. They are available for free over the phone or online. If the property is listed for lease, the agent or the landlord should have them or be able to get them.

8.   Make sure you have good signage for your studio. Bad signage will kill your business before it starts. Make sure your sign not only looks good on paper, but will also be legible from the vehicles driving by your studio at 40 MPH from several hundred feet away.

Information like household size, household income, age, education, and other facts are called demographics. They are available for free if you know where to look. One such resource is available if you become a free member of LoopNet, loopnet.com. LoopNet is a commercial real estate listing service used by real estate companies and property owners to market their properties. Every listing on LoopNet has a free demographic report you can access. Find any property in a neighborhood you are interesting in and use the demographic report from there to find the information you need. Any good commercial real estate agent will be happy to provide you with demographic reports, as will many chambers of commerce and economic development offices. The government website census.gov is also a great free resource, but it is a little more difficult to navigate than LoopNet. You can also purchase a demographic report online from numerous providers.

Don't let demographics complicate or confuse you. All they are is a tool to give you a picture of certain factors and characteristics. Use that data to help lead you to where you should be. In business lingo, the neighborhood or area you want to serve is your "trade area" or your "market area." A demographic report usually defines a trade area by zip code; by a set distance from your location like a one, three, or five mile radius; or by the "drive time" away from your property. All are only useful to the point of how far your customer will actually travel to do business with you. If you are the only studio in a thirty-mile radius, you can draw customers from a longer distance in a way you couldn't do if there are studios on every corner. Sometimes interstates, railroad tracks, parks, and large tracts of land can be barriers in a trade area that customers won't cross. Use your knowledge of the area and your common sense to determine what your trade area is, then order your report accordingly. Become familiar with the data within that area.

When working with demographics, always compare the data they report for an area with the average data of that type for the same region. For instance: if the demographic report says that within one mile of your area the average household income is $58,000 per year and the average household income for the county is $48,000, then you know you are dealing with an upper-middle class neighborhood. If that same report said the household income within two miles of your location was $115,000 per year, then you know you are near a wealthy neighborhood.

Your competition & market research

When selecting a location, don't be afraid to locate near competition. Before you do, make sure you know who and what your competition does, and what you will do differently or better. Having competition in a market could be a good indicator of a good place to do business, especially if they can't handle the business they have, or if the market is big enough for multiple martial arts studios. Of course, there is nothing wrong with being the only studio in a hot area either!

Back when I was a real estate broker I did some work for the largest local BP Amoco Convenience Store operator. He had a high performing store at a top traffic intersection in our metro area. A year after this store opened my business partner represented his client, QuikTrip, in putting a large convenience store one block away. My BP Amoco client was ready to kill me! He accused me of unethical behavior, since my partner worked with his competition to put a competing store so close. I told him to not lose faith--his operation was different than QuikTrip, he had a better location, and most importantly he had a car wash and they didn't.

A year later I bumped into him and he apologized. I was curious why. He said "my business increased 17 percent since QuikTrip opened." Clearly. this was a case that competition helped draw more customers to the area, and everyone made more money. In real estate development this concept is called a "node." This is why motels, fast food, and hotels all try to locate near each other. They do more business together than they do apart. Plus, you want to locate in an area that is healthy, vibrant, and can support more business.

Once you identify your competition, visit them. If your area doesn't have competition go to the nearest studios and the most successful studios. Check them out. Observe their layout, look, hours, prices, services, flyers, cleanliness, and the vibe you get from their operation. Are they friendly? Why are people doing business with them? What is their "purple cow?"

To find out these things stop in during their business hours and act like you are a new potential customer wanting the tour. How is their sales technique? What is their sales technique? What can you learn from them that will help you? What equipment do they provide? What equipment do they sell? Are there wall-to-wall mirrors? How did they decorate? How many classes per week are there? Do they offer classes by age group, ability level, or are they all open? What is the maximum ability they can train to or certify for? Do they have any specials for new customers? How do they handle their billing? Do they have any way to follow up from your visit?—

For every question you ask them make sure you have an answer for the very same question about your own studio when you are ready to open. Having those answers will make you better prepared and a better business operator.

You may or may not want to let your competition know you are opening a studio. If they have too much business then perhaps you can pay them a referral fee for any customers they send your way. If you don't think you are direct competition with each other, you can let them know your intentions. Let your "gut" lead you. Perhaps you can ask them the pros and cons of having a martial arts studio. You never know, you may have found a mentor to help you walk through the process.

Take what they say with a grain of salt. They might not welcome competition, so they may try to scare you out of your dream. You have the street smarts to know when someone is bluffing you or not.

Be open to the possibility that if you let them know you are considering getting in the business, you may find out that they want to sell theirs or have you take it over for a reasonable amount of money. Remember that you have not because you ask not!

For every competitor make a file on them that includes a list of everything you learned about them and update it from time to time. Take a map of your area, and note the location of your competition. *Congratulations!* You have just completed "market research." The only thing missing from a true market research study are facts and figures to estimate the demand for your goods and services. That's where the demographic report comes in handy. However, never let a report get in the way of basic common sense, but always be careful.

Your space

For a martial arts studio, select a space that is about 1,000 - 2,000 Square Feet (SF) of mostly open floor plan, with restrooms and some office space. Make sure it is properly zoned for your use. If not a complaining neighbor can shut you down later. A good real estate agent or landlord will know the zoning, but you can always confirm with your city's zoning department online or on the telephone. Make sure you are on a street with good traffic, that's easy to get to, with signage for your business which can be seen, with abundant parking, and close and convenient for your target customer. _Do not compromise on any of those elements_ no matter how good of a deal it may appear to be. Don't worry about providing lockers or showers unless it is an absolute business necessity in your market.

Get space in a building that is clean, well-lit, and evokes feelings of credibility, professionalism, and safety. It doesn't have to be fancy or expensive but it does need to reflect the excellence and professionalism you will provide your customers. When you lease space make sure the landlord and other tenants won't have issues with your hours of operation and the parking spaces your customers will take. Adequate parking will make or break any business. Most of your parking demands will be in the evening so a property that has a full parking lot during the day might have a lot of parking when you need it. Try to get ground floor space if you can, but this is not as critical as the other factors are if your market is hot enough.

BARRY'S STORY:
My friend "Barry" was a Marine. After he completed his tour of duty, he thought "wouldn't it be great to find a way to get paid doing something I love?" He loved to fight and teach, and Barry recognized a need for quality martial arts training in the military town he lived in. He got together with three of his Marine buddies who shared his vision. They opened a martial arts studio near the base. Their only advertising was word-of-mouth. They located their studio on a busy street and had good signage and a banner to promote their business. They were busy nearly from the start, but it took them two years before they were profitable. I always recommend spending ample money to promote your business, especially at the start.

To open they had:
- A 1,200 SF +/- studio, mostly open except for 2 offices and restrooms.
- Wrestling mats.
- They developed their own curriculum and training programs that mirrored the martial arts industry.
- Lots of "Karategi" (judo uniforms, a.k.a "Gi") for the customers to buy.
- Foot wear for customers to buy.
- Shin pads.
- Building signage.
- A banner.
- A website.
- A desk, computer, phone, multi-function printer, internet, email, and business cards.

Their total opening investment was about $5,000, including utility and security deposits, and rent. It would've been a lot higher, but the partners took no salary until the operation was strong enough to afford to pay themselves wages.

Each class they offered lasted two hours. They offered four classes daily, seven days a week and a customer could attend up to three classes per week of their choice. They had classes in self-defense and traditional martial arts. They grossed about $9,000/month, and their operating expenses, including salaries to themselves, were about $5,000/month. Their profit was over $4,000/month, doing something they loved!!

Barry was successful because he found a business that fit his passions. He is a great people person, and he knows the value of great communication skills and loyalty to his customers. He feels his greatest selling point is his patience. A patient, skilled teacher who loves people and loves teaching will make or break a business. Barry's patience, friendliness, and team's skill were what made his business unique.

Here are some tips from Barry on being successful in a martial arts studio, and in life:

1. The reason most people are afraid to learn to fight is they don't like falling. Falling is a necessary part of fighting, and life. The key to martial arts is to learn to fall right and to get back up after you fall. If you fall wrong in martial arts you injure yourself. If you fall wrong in life--in

ways like not learning from your mistakes, not taking a risk again, or not trying to grow or better yourself--then you also injure yourself.

2.   Teach people to trust themselves and let them learn it's OK to fall and how to fall. Once the fear of falling is overcome and they learn to fall and not get hurt, then real learning and progress can occur.

3.   Offer something your competition doesn't. That is your "unique selling proposition" (USP) also known as your "purple cow." Include your USP into your elevator speech.

Here is Barry's elevator speech as to what his martial arts studio does: Barry provides world class fitness and self-defense instruction through their unique blend of friendliness, skill, and patience. Their passion is to teach individuals, families, and kids martial arts in a way that promotes a positive lifestyle.

4.   Work with your competition, and don't be afraid to refer business to them if a prospective customer checks you out and doesn't immediately sign up. You and your competition can benefit from referring customers to each other. Because you were positive and professional, and tried to meet the needs of the customer, usually after the customer tries the competition they often come back and stay.

5.   People like free things so give them a free group lesson and a free one-on-one session. Barry would use this technique, with no pressure selling, to let people try a class. Parents brought their kids in to try a class and would stay to watch how Barry and his team handled the class and their kids. Seeing their care, patience, and how much fun they made the class caused the parents to trust and respect Barry's operation. Barry would offer the parents a free session to an adult class and often Barry would sign up the whole family for training, all from one free class he gave away!

6.   Make learning fun, and always be patient with the students no matter their age or education level.

Barry's martial arts studio earned a good reputation in their community for quality training in self-defense. Because of this they were contacted to provide personal security at special events and clubs around town. This is how they launched a very profitable security company earning an additional $20,000 per month.

Check the Success Snapshot of "Personal Security Services" for the rest of Barry's story of how he used his martial arts studio to launch another successful business.

> *"It's OK to fall down -*
> *You have to learn to fall right to fight."*
>
> *-Barry*

SUCCESS SNAPSHOT

LAWN MOWING / LAWNCARE

"Farming Is Fun!!"

Believe it or not, these are two totally different businesses. Often people will start a lawn mowing service by themselves that grows into a lawn care company with employees. Keep that in mind in this chapter as I highlight their differences. Lawn mowing can be a great source of extra income. Many lawn services also do snow removal, which is mentioned briefly below, and is the topic of the next Success Snapshot.

Lawn care often leads to extra work and extra income like:

Landscaping	Hedge trimming
Sprinkler sales/service	Window cleaning
Power washing	Deck cleaning and staining
Cleaning gutters	Snow removal
Maintaining flower beds	Cleaning up dog waste
Home repairs	Tree trimming or removal

The sky is the limit for services you can perform once you earn your customer's trust. Just don't get distracted from your main money-making tasks. For any extra work requested that you cannot perform, have referral fees set up with reputable companies.

The income estimates below do not include extra revenue from extra services and referrals. As always these estimates are not guaranteed and are for discussion purposes only. They will vary widely based on your market and the time and effort you put into your business. These income estimates and the list of tools needed to start were provided from my friend "Ben" who helped with this Success Snapshot.

	Lawn Mowing	Lawn Care	Snow Removal
Income Range:	$25k - $50k/year	$50k - $250k +/year	$65-$125/hour
Start Up Costs:	$500 - $1000	$20,000 - $40,000	$3k-$5k/ truck

TRAINING REQUIRED: A basic knowledge of lawn care; care for shrubs, bushes, plants; training in snow removal if you plow snow.

SPECIAL SKILLS: Small engine service and repair, ability to apply fertilizers, ability to service sprinklers.

LICENSING REQUIRED: None to mow, but some states and cities require training or licenses for applying fertilizers and chemicals.

PHYSICAL REQUIREMENTS: Able to lift 100#, operate mowers, bend, stoop, and be in the sun/outdoors for long periods of time.

NEED TO INCORPORATE: Not required but recommended when you can afford it.

EQUIPMENT NEEDED:
Whether you work alone, or for each crew you put in the field, you will need the following:

- A reliable pickup truck, with 4-wheel drive and a tow package. Get the best you can afford so you can make a good first impression and build customer confidence in your business.

- A drop deck or low rise trailer. Use portable ramps with your truck until you can afford a trailer.

- A good commercial-grade lawn mower. My friend Ben (story below) recommends the Hustler X-1 and John Deere Zero Turning Radius mowers, along with a 36"-walk-behind Ferris mower. Ben strongly recommends the extra accessories of a stripe kit and a bagger when you can afford them, for a more finished look.

- An aerator if you offer aeration. (You can rent it as needed also.)

- At least (4) 5-gallon gas cans: three regular gas, one mixed gas.

- Leaf blowers and weed trimmers and lots of reel (Ben recommends Shindiah Red Max trimmers and blowers).

- On-vehicle lockable tool bin.

- Trash bags, rags, sun block, bug spray, cooler, water, and Gatorade.

- Stihl chainsaw and hedge trimmers are recommended by Ben.

- Hedge clippers, Hand tools and a cordless drill.

- Three bank bags for under the truck seat.

- A 2-ton jack, air compressor, and extra tires for your mower(s).

When you can afford it, you should buy extra parts of all of your equipment and have at least one extra of each type with you out in the field or with each crew. Your equipment will wear out and break: usually while you are trying to mow the last ten lawns before it rains!

At your shop, garage, or storage area, keep a mat and containers for changing oil. There are companies that will buy, or accept, your used oil. Check in your area for oil recycling companies. Have tools and a grinder to sharpen your own blades. Sharpening your blades daily is a must: your yards will look better, your customers will be happier, and you can mow yards quicker, making you more money. Finally, have set up racks and bins so you can be well organized from the start. You will make a lot more money mowing yards than you will wasting time looking for misplaced tools or spending money replacing tools you can't find. If your shop and trucks are organized you will give a professional impression to your customers and employees. People will notice, and it will matter.

Check with your State Department of Revenue: many states give a full or partial rebate on gas taxes paid for the gasoline used in mowers and trimmers. Over a mowing season this can add up to thousands coming back to you. That extra money is reason enough to save all receipts and do paper work to track the gas going into vehicles vs. equipment.

BEN'S STORY:

My friend "Ben" is a seasoned lawn and snow removal professional. He's been in the business more than fifteen years, and his personal income tops $200k/year. You will love his story.

Ben started his own lawn service from scratch at a cost of $15,000. He was profitable immediately. After a couple of years he grew to service twenty-five lawns and was able to buy a struggling turnkey lawn service with 150 lawns for $40k. The price equaled three months of gross income for the business which is standard price to pay for lawn services.

He got a bank loan for the whole amount and had it paid within months. First Ben had to fix the messes the company he bought had created. I believe we make money by solving problems, but sometimes it's easier to start from scratch than fix someone else's problems. Ben took the company, fixed the problems, and built something very nice from it, with a lot of work.

Ben focused his efforts on being the best lawn and snow company serving specific subdivisions and businesses. He tried to keep all of his work centered in specific areas with higher household incomes and higher property values.

Whether you want to build a big lawn care company, or just go out and mow lawns, the principles and steps to achieve growth are the same. To start his business Ben had obtained insurance, bonding, Chamber of Commerce and Better Business Bureau memberships, and local city licensing for his business. He included "Licensed, Bonded, and Insured Member of the Chamber of Commerce and BBB" on his professional looking cards, flyers, and advertising. He says promoting that was a key in getting new business.

Earlier I wrote "all marketing is personal." Ben's success is a great example of personal marketing for businesses. To launch, Ben selected the area he wanted to service. He knocked on every door in the neighborhood, meeting people and making a good, friendly impression on potential customers. In sales and marketing this is called "farming a territory." He tried to avoid homes with chain link fences. He especially liked mowing duplex townhomes. He usually charged $35/mow, bagged and trimmed, for the average sized yard, for a house or duplex townhome. If he could get both sides of a duplex, he would chop the price to $25/mow for each side. He could usually mow a property in about 15 minutes. If you keep your yards within close-by neighborhoods you can focus your time on production, instead of driving all over for work. Of course, you have to go where your business is. Your first customer may not be in the prime target areas you want to be in. No matter, if it is profitable and gets you started, you can farm for customers wherever.

Ben developed a good rapport and reputation with his customers from the start by personally ensuring their lawns were mowed to the highest standards. He trains his workers to go the extra mile for customers. If toys were in the yard or the newspaper was in the street, Ben's workers would courteously move these items for the customer. He didn't "nickel and dime" them on occasional extras either.

Ben maintains a high standard with his workers. They are trained not only to mow lawns, but to have good customer relations. He allows his workers to wear shorts, but tank tops or shirtless workers are not allowed. He prefers to provide them sleeved tee shirts, lime green or orange, with his company logo and information on it. It's a consistent professional look, and it lets the customer know the people walking around in their yard are from their lawn company.

Ben invoices on the last day of the month by having his staff leave envelopes with statements at the customer's residence, which saves on mailing. Ben will email their statements if the customer prefers. Workers keep the customer envelopes in a bank bag in their truck, along with each day's list of lawns to mow, with workers' notes on them, which they turn in for management and billing. One bank bag is used for expenses (Ben will give cash, and replenish with receipts); the other is used for customer check and cash collections.

Later Ben used Google AdWords and bought an ad for an "AAA Better Business Bureau Rated Lawn Service" in his hometown. Unknown to Ben a national maintenance company happened to be looking for a reputable snow removal vendor for a major retailer. They contacted Ben and are currently paying him a $4k/month retainer for each of the five stores he plows for them during five months of winter. That's $100,000 folks!

When you want to expand into commercial accounts or snow removal, take the same farming approach as you did with building residential accounts. Instead of selecting a target subdivision, identify potential properties to service in your targeted market areas and "farm" them. Make a flyer just for your commercial accounts and start contacting them. Avoid doing a direct mail campaign as they are expensive and typically only receive a 1 percent +/- response rate. Make every effort to talk directly to the owner or the person who makes decisions regarding grounds maintenance. You will have better luck talking to owners than you might think. Most businesses are always looking to save money or get better service.

Ben found these have been great sources of new commercial and residential lawn and snow accounts:

1. Servicing bank-owned foreclosed homes. Contact a bank and ask for their Property Management or R.E.O. (real estate owned) department and tell them you want to bid on the lawn care of their foreclosed properties. Ask them what they're willing to pay for their lawns to be mowed. Most banks will be anxious to talk to you as handling empty foreclosed houses is a great inconvenience for them. If you take good care of them, they will happily call you first. Also ask them who handles home clean-outs of foreclosed properties. This is a very lucrative source of year-round side income that you can earn if you develop a good relationship with the decision maker.

2. Mowing for HUD and VA homes for sale (and their cleanouts). Contact your local office to find out who handles grounds maintenance of homes for sale.
   f

3. Military bases, prisons, government Facilities, and the Army Corps of Engineers may have mowing contracts. Many federal contracts are offered through the website fedbizopps.gov. Check it out to see what and how to bid.

4. Mowing a cemetery. Contact whoever is the custodian or seller of plots there, and ask if you can bid on the lawn care. Ben makes $22,000 per year mowing one cemetery for three hours per trip on his off day.

5. Subcontracting for cities, counties, and states. They often contract out mowing and snow removal of their right of way, parks, properties in violation of "weed and litter" ordinances, and special projects. Contact their purchasing, contracting, code enforcement, or public works departments directly for information on how to bid on these opportunities.

6. Contact property management companies, national maintenance companies, homeowner's associations, apartment complexes, retirement homes, office buildings, shopping centers, and any building owner of a property you want to mow. Find out when they solicit bids and how to submit them. Many bids are "fill in the blank" forms. Many companies will ask for bids late summer or early fall for the next year for budgeting purposes.

7. Contact retail and restaurant chains via their main website or through their local manager or regional offices. Their property management, real estate, or purchasing department should be able to get you information on how to bid.

Once you have earned a good customer relationship it's easy to get your customers' snow removal work. Ben markets to current customers for clearing their driveways, stoops, and sidewalks. He generally charges $45 per time and it takes about fifteen minutes per house to do. Snow removal is a <u>great</u> source of extra income, as you will learn when you read the next Success Snapshot.

SUCCESS SNAPSHOT

SNOW REMOVAL

"Feasibility: Is the Juice Worth The Squeeze?"

INCOME: $65-$125/hour or more, per truck *if* it snows. You can make extra money salting and sanding also.

START-UP COSTS: $1k - $5k cost per suitable truck. This assumes you have a reliable 4x4 truck, heavy duty preferred, with an automatic transmission.

EXPERIENCE/TRAINING: None other than snow removal and driving aptitude.

LICENSING: Driver's license

SPECIAL SKILLS: Must like working long hours, often overnight, and be able to drive in bad snowy weather.

NEED TO INCORPORATE: No, but insurance is a must!

Many lawn services, landscapers, trucking companies, tree services, cement companies, and other construction trades who slow down during the winter have found that snow removal is a perfect way to earn extra money in the off season. You already have a truck or trucks, a phone line, and paid overhead to keep your business alive over the winter, so why not use your off-time to earn extra income with resources and equipment you mostly already have?

You could get paid big money to plow parking lots, homeowner's driveways, or be a snow removal subcontractor for your city, county, state, homeowner's association, or another snow removal contractor. Decide up-front the type of snow removal business you want to perform. Consider factors like the time the snow is to be removed, the rates you can charge, and the customers you will serve. Not knowing the type of snow removal contracts you want and getting stuck in contracts that are burdensome will be a problem for you. For instance: most businesses want their parking lots cleaned before they open. Most cities, counties, and states want their roads cleared as soon as possible also. Sometimes the timing of the snowfall works in your favor for this, sometimes it doesn't. Residential customers and apartment complexes usually don't want to be plowed overnight as the noise could wake them or their neighbors up.

Make sure you can service the contracts you commit to before you get yourself too spread (and stressed) out. Even though snow removal is not your main business, your reputation is still on the line and you don't want to cause problems with customers and hurt your good name.

Start looking for commercial snow removal contracts late summer or early fall. Most importantly: let your existing customers know you offer snow removal services and personally ask for the chance to bid their work. You can earn even more money by salting or sanding their walks and drives. If they like you or your work in your main business, chances are they will like your snow removal also. Bid snow removal work like you would any other service. Give your customer a proposal or an estimate customized to their name and location. Be specific about the charges and how you will bill. If they commit to you, ask them to sign the contract and make sure you give them one and keep one for your file.

Try to maintain your contracts within a specific neighborhood. This helps you increase profit and reduce wasted time driving around. If the business is lucrative enough or the customer important enough, you can take snow removal contracts that aren't in the same neighborhoods. Use your best judgment and common sense to decide what you should do.

You can charge by the hour, by the depth of the snowfall, or a set amount each time you plow their property. You can even get a set retainer paid to you each month, like the $20,000 per month my friend Ben gets whether it snows or not. This is a great way for a property owner to know what to budget for snow removal, and it gives you guaranteed income. Your market will dictate what to charge. Do some market research to find out what other snow removal contractors are charging by being a "mystery shopper" and ask them about their rates and services.

Ben plows many of his lawn customers' snow. He brings a worker with him to blow the sidewalks and shovel the front entrance while he plows the driveway, all of which takes about 10 minutes. He charges $45 each time for the average property.

Get as good of a blade as you can afford on your truck. Of course the best time to buy a used blade is in the spring or summer. A used blade starts at about $1,000 and they can go up to around $5,000 for a top-of-the-line new blade. Ben uses a Hiniker blade, fully equipped with a pair of guide poles and over-the-blade lights. If properly maintained a blade has about a twenty-year life expectancy.

Ben only uses vehicles with automatic transmissions. He says if you're doing snow removal plan on rebuilding your truck's transmission every fifteen months at a cost of about $2,500. This includes a one-year warranty, which you likely will use. A reputable shop should be able to rebuild your transmission in a day. Plan on the transmission rebuild as a cost of doing business for every truck you plow with.

Also contact schools/school districts, churches, apartment complexes, condominium and townhome regimes, grocery stores, property management companies, real estate companies, hotels, shopping centers, and your local city, county, and state offices to find out how to bid their work, and who to talk to. You can farm an area, use Craigslist, and Google AdWords to promote your snow removal.

Is it right for me?
How do you know if you should invest the time and money to be able to offer snow removal services? Answering that question will demonstrate if a business is feasible. "Feasible" is a fancy way that bankers, accountants, and lawyers use to say "does it make sense to make that investment," or as I like to say: "is the juice worth the squeeze?"

To see if snow removal is feasible, go online and research the average snowfall for the winter in your area along with the number of snowfalls or snow events that your area averages. You can Google this, go to the National Weather Service, or check with your local County Extension Office. Even the Chamber of Commerce and your local economic development office should have this information.

Next, take how many customers you think you will get times what you will charge them and multiply that total by the average snowfalls or snow amounts and you will get a rough idea of what your gross earnings doing snow removal over the winter will be. Try to be as realistic as you can, and not overly hopeful, when you guess the number of customers and your charge to them. You want to avoid unpleasant surprises as much as possible. By doing this exercise you just learned how to forecast (another banker term), or predict, your income. That is an important step in managing the growth of your business.

Now take your gross income you just estimated and subtract your initial investment to start snow removal, the planned transmission rebuild, and the operating expenses for performing the snow removal. Then ask yourself if the amount of money left over is worth the investment and effort to plow snow. In other words, is the juice worth the squeeze?

If you are a lawn service or other company that typically doesn't work over the winter, you still have to pay to keep your equipment and vehicles insured and your phones on whether you work or not. So except for the costs of extra labor and fuel, plus the cost of equipment and planned transmission rebuilding, you may find that snow removal is a great way to help get you and your guys through the winter.

At least now you have an intelligent way to see if the investment and effort makes sense, instead of just guessing. As a bonus, you learned how to project, or predict, your income from a business activity as well.

Before you start any business an important step is to do a month-by-month forecast of income and expenses for at least one or preferably two years. This will help show you feasibility and what to plan for. I have forms for doing this in the Business Plan Checklist™ and on the website illegaltolegal.org.

SUCCESS SNAPSHOT

LAUNDROMAT

"We Make Money By Solving Problems"

*"To Be A Neighborhood Business,
You Have To Be A Good Neighbor"*

INCOME: $30,000 - $75,000/year or more per location depending on the size of your store and your overhead. This can vary widely if you have more equipment or have extra services like dry cleaning or drop off laundry.

SPECIAL SKILLS: A little mechanical knowledge of commercial washers and dryers is helpful. This is easily obtained from the owner's manuals and field practice while using basic hand tools.

EXPERIENCE: None required.

LICENSING: None required.

THINGS TO READ TO HELP YOU START: *Coin-Op Magazine.*

Over the years, and as part of researching and writing this book, I've talked to a lot of people about many different businesses. Pretty much everyone thought a laundromat was a good business and most said they would like to eventually own one. These same people also say they want to own a car wash and apartment building as well. Go figure.

There are four ways to make money in the laundry business:

1.   Operating a self-service laundromat without an attendant (worker) onsite. You still need to arrange for janitorial as well as opening and closing of the store. The opening and closing can be done automatically with a special lock and timer if you choose.

2.   Operating a self-service laundromat with an attendant onsite. This is different than the unattended laundry as the attendant can directly oversee the store plus take in loads of laundry for extra income. These loads of laundry are called "drop off laundry." You need to have a larger store, a lot of volume, or charge a lot of money to be able to afford attendants so be careful if you pursue this option.

3.   Owning and providing laundry equipment in apartment buildings. Under this scenario the building owner or landlord provides the space, utilities, and cleaning at no charge and the laundry operator provides the coin operated machines and equipment maintenance. The operator and landlord split the income which the operator collects and reports to the landlord regularly. I've seen the split go from 30/70, landlord/operator, to 60/40 depending on whether the laundry is high or low volume, if you provide new or used equipment, and if the landlord gets a signing bonus for a long-term contract. The usual split is 50/50. Many laundry equipment distributors have contracts to provide laundries to the big apartment complexes, but apartment buildings too small for the big boys are a great opportunity if you want to go this route.

4.   Operating a uniform, linen, or diaper service. Unless you have some big customers already lined up, national and regional companies make it difficult to enter this market.

This is a special story for me, for it is one of my own. Over a two-year period my (then) wife and I opened a laundromat and we were so successful we expanded to four more stores by reinvesting the profits and finding problem laundromats to acquire. After those two years we sold the five stores for about a $100,000 profit plus what we made while we operated them. First let me share with you how I fell into the laundry business.

As a then real estate broker I used to do property management. I managed a small storefront commercial building in a working class Latino neighborhood for a client. This building had a 750 square foot (SF) laundromat in it. It was a nasty, nasty place! Equipment was old and didn't work, it had a bad roach problem, the space was constantly vandalized, it had gang graffiti in it, and customers were afraid to use this laundromat. It essentially died on the vine from neglect and was available for lease.

I grew up around there and knew this neighborhood was vibrant and growing. The building was on the main drag. Since this space was already equipped for laundry, I figured all it needed was remodeling and new equipment. Doing all of the plumbing and electrical for a new laundromat is *very* expensive, like $50,000 to $100,000 +. I negotiated a lease for us to open the laundromat subject to our ability to get the bank loan we needed for renovation and equipment.

Little did I know that jumping into the laundry business would give me the second rule of Pelshaw's Principles of Profitable Business which says:

> *"Make money by solving problems."*
> *-Pelshaw's Principles of Profitable Business*

The complete list is found in Section Three and on the website illegaltolegal.org. The old laundromat was a problem. It needed an extensive makeover including remodeling, new equipment, even new management. I was asked this question a lot: if it was such a great business, then why was it left to die on the vine? Was it worth getting into? To answer that question I needed a way to accurately predict what I could make on the venture. At first I had no idea how to calculate what our income could be. Would we be able to make enough from the laundry to make the loan payment, all expenses, and profit?

Why did I want a laundromat there? Within two miles of us there were 50,000 people and our competition was two other old dilapidated smaller laundries. I figured there was great market potential. I checked the wash and dry prices on our competition and the equipment they had. I priced my machines accordingly. I was going to be the most expensive of the laundries in our market, but I was the only one with new equipment in a remodeled store, and I offered the most dryers.

Normally if you buy a business you ask to review several years of the actual revenue and expenses and tax returns of a business. That process is called "due diligence" in banker and attorney lingo. That wasn't possible here so we had to make our own projections. But how? Our business would be very different from the previous laundromat there but we still didn't know how much money it would make.

I talked to different people to help us accurately predict the expected revenue. Our first contact was the laundry equipment distributor. He was well-meaning, but he had no clue how to project income with anything better than a guess. I could guess! Besides, he had a vested interest in trying to sell us equipment, so I needed to get an answer from someone not making money on my purchase. Before we spent money we didn't have we needed something more than a guess.

I talked to other business people, not in the laundry business, and they suggested I take my gross income--the income of the store if all equipment was operating 100 percent for the complete time it was open-- and then research to find out what the average percentage of time the equipment was being used. The fancy way to say that, in "banker and lawyer talk" is "what was the average utilization of the equipment?"

The laundry distributor told me at the time the average laundromat nationally averaged an 18 percent equipment utilization factor. We felt based on population and lack of good competition in the area that we could achieve a 20 percent utilization factor. We actually achieved a 21.5 percent average utilization in that first store, but more on that later.

The equipment distributor helped me by letting me know that the top load machines, if operating 100 percent of the time, could do three separate loads in an hour, and the front loader could do two loads in an hour. So to figure out what the income potential was all I had to do was to take the price to operate the equipment, piece by piece, multiplied by the number of loads per hour, for the number of hours we were open per day, times the number of days in the month to come up with our gross potential income. Here's the math we came up with:

(20) Top load washers x 3 loads/hour x $1.00/load =
$60 per hour gross potential income from the top load washers

(1) front load washer x 2 loads/hour x $3.00/load =
$6 per hour gross potential income from the front load washer

(14) dryers x $0.25/drying cycle x 5 cycles/hour =
$17.50 per hour gross potential income from the dryers

TOTAL HOURLY GROSS POTENTIAL INCOME:
$60/hr. + $6/hr. + $17.50/hr. = $83.50/hour

$83.50/hour x 14 hours of daily operation =
$1,169/day gross potential income
$1,169/day X 30 days in a month
= $35,070 mo. gross potential income
* 0.18 utilization factor
= **$6,302.60 Est. Gross Monthly Income**

We didn't know that after the first ninety days we averaged a 0.215 utilization factor which equaled $7,540 per month in actual gross income. From there we subtracted our loan payment and expenses and realized $3,500/month profit for about one or two hours of work a day.

The first three months were the scariest as we didn't have much business, even though I had a banner in front and regularly distributed bilingual flyers around the neighborhood. I remember coming home one day with my wife sitting at the table with her calculator, in shock, telling me how many quarters it took to make our monthly loan payment. Needless to say a smile wasn't on her face when we were having that conversation!

Our first store was close to our home, so I made it a point to check it frequently. If there were customers there I would go up to them, introduce myself, thank them for their business, and make friendly chit-chat. One time after doing this I was thirsty so I opened up our soda vending machine and pulled a soda out. Then I had an idea: I went up to the customer I was just visiting with and asked what soda she liked. The lady had a strange look on her face but told me her choice. A moment later I came back with a soda and told her "Thank you very much for your business. We appreciate it. Make sure you tell your friends about us." Other times I would give people free dryer sheets, put extra time on the dryers, or I gave them a free wash.

I believe if you are to be a neighborhood business you first have to be a good neighbor. It was a lot of fun surprising people with random acts of kindness. I was very sincere about trying to show appreciation for their business. If they would talk to me, and most would, I would try to get their first name. When they came back (they almost always did) I made sure I gave them a cheerful "Hello, how are you doing?" and call them by their name.

Most laundry customers, at least for laundries in the "hood," weren't upscale people. A lot of them were barely making it paycheck to paycheck or welfare check to welfare check. Based on the last owner of this laundromat the customers weren't used to being appreciated or respected. Whenever I had the chance, I would tell people that my single mother raised us seven kids on welfare, and even though I was the youngest I was the first one to conventionally graduate high school, go to college, and be successfully self-employed. They liked the fact that I was like them, didn't talk down to them, that I lived in the neighborhood, and I worked hard to keep it a nice place for them.

Just because our clients were poor I never treated them like they were poor. I made sure they had shiny new working equipment in a clean well lit professional environment where they felt appreciated and welcomed. If a mom had a handful of clothes and a handful of kids I would help her bring her clothes in or ask her permission to give her kids some little candy treats we kept on hand for just such occasions. Do little things for your customers to be a nice person and show appreciation and respect. Cleanliness, new equipment, and being a good neighbor was my purple cow in the laundry business.

The first ninety days were financially scary but then it was like a switch turned on. It was insane how busy our little laundromat became. That little 750 SF store was regularly producing $7,500/month in business. That's about $100/SF per month in sales. After utilities, rent, insurance, supplies, and our loan payment, we cleared $3,500 a month! Since it was too small to justify having workers, we ran it as a self-service unattended laundromat. To save money I did all of the cleaning and the opening and closing of the store myself which gave me a chance to visit with my regular customers.

I opened at 6 a.m. and did our last load at 9 p.m., meaning we closed at 10 p.m. On days we were busy, like the weekend, I usually popped into the laundromat once or twice a day to make sure everything was working and clean. Nothing would kill business in a coin-operated laundry faster than the change machine being empty or not working, or your store being a mess!

We used a Small Business Administration (SBA) loan of $70,000 to open the first store. With that we:
- Installed new washers and dryers.
- Installed a new change machine and soap machine.
- Air conditioned the space.
- Repainted and refurbished the space.
- Installed a new floor.
- Got a new sign.
- Paid for the "now open" banner and flyers we distributed.
- Paid for a zoned security alarm system with a vibration sensor like what's on safe doors for the change machine. With the zones we kept the alarm on the change machine and the back room door during business hours, and then all the zones were turned on when we locked up. Several times this kept thieves and vandals from trying to steal the change machine during operating hours.

Here are two funny stories about owning a laundromat. My friends would always tease me that as a laundry owner I must pay for everything in quarters "wink, wink." They assumed since it was a cash business they thought I took cash and spent it instead of reporting it for income tax purposes. Well, they were close but not completely right. Yes, we got a lot of quarters, which we put back in the change machine. I took the dollars in the change machine and spent those, but not until I logged them on our daily sheet.

I remember going to the grocery store and paying with a stack of one dollar bills. Some friendly cashiers asked me if I was a waiter since I had so many one dollar bills. I told them I owned laundromats. One flirty and very funny cashier once asked me if I was a male stripper!! WOW that made me feel good! I then spontaneously came up with one of my best one-line responses yet: I told her I was a reverse stripper - that my wife paid me to put my clothes back on!!

I logged every penny to come in the business, even though I paid taxes on it, so that I could prove income and value when I went to sell the business. Since we don't know what the future holds, you should always run your business so you can increase and maximize the value of the business, either for loan purposes or for sale. The daily cash logs matched our bank deposits and our books, so we could well prove the income our business generated. Being able to prove income is crucial if you ever want to get a loan or get the best sales price should you ever sell it. At the same time I logged all the income, I was aggressive about taking write-offs. But beware as too many write-offs can hurt the value and bankability of your business too.

I did spend a lot of the cash from the laundry business. There's nothing illegal about spending cash, just keep receipts for cash spent on business purposes and report all of your income.

Later, we sold a laundromat to "Rusty" who was certain that I was pocketing money and not reporting all of the income. He was smart: he requested two years utility bills, tax returns, and bank statements from us to prove the income we told him the business produced. If you buy an existing laundry, or any existing business, request those same things as well. This is called "due diligence" in banker and lawyer lingo. Most sellers will give you enough time to perform your due diligence. Walk away from the deal if they don't give you enough time, lie to you, or hide answers from you.

As a rule of thumb most laundromats use about 15-20 percent +/- of their income for utility bills, so knowing the utility costs could help you estimate what a store (even your competitor's store) is producing cash-wise.

Even at the closing table Rusty didn't believe me that we didn't pocket any income. Two months after the purchase was final he called me up and told me that part of him was happy and part of him was mad at me. He discovered that the business was performing exactly as I said it would and that there was no extra income. I then asked him why was he mad at me. Rusty said he was hoping I was lying about reporting all of the income. He was so pleased with my stores that he bought two more from me, purchasing three of the five stores I sold.

Other than the cash flow and the condition of the equipment, the next most significant factor that helped me get top dollar for the sale of the stores were the leases I had for each location. Each lease was for at least five or seven years which matched the term of our bank loans or equipment leases. Each lease also had at least three (3) five-year options to renew. The landlords and I agreed to reasonable rental increases, either 3 percent per year or 10-12 percent every five years. Having the lease with the options gave me control of the laundries for twenty years +/-. I could've done a shorter term lease, but I wanted to control the space so that I couldn't lose my lease like the guy did where we made our first store. Having the longer lease gave us value when we went to sell the business.

A secret for wealth creation is for every lease we signed we also built in an option to purchase the property we were leasing, plus a "first right of refusal" for any legitimate offer that the seller would accept. A first right of refusal means that if the seller accepts an offer they have to give you the first chance to buy it on the same terms. Make sure your leases have both clauses in them.

Many people think when they go to start a new business that they need to own the real estate. That's great if you can afford it but I think a smarter way to do it is to get the business open, then use the profits from the business to purchase the real estate when you can afford it. That's why having an option to purchase the building you are leasing is important if you can get it. You can always negotiate the lowest purchase price on a building when it is empty and not producing rent for the landlord. Once you go in and remodel, put new equipment in, and build up a good business, many landlords will get greedy and will raise a purchase price, or not sell it to you at all. Having the option built into your lease becomes more important to you or to a future owner if you sell your business.

Another lesson I learned from being in the laundry business applies to any business. When you get into business, often you're working long hours every day without a break or anyone to cover for you. Many well-meaning people leave a great job with benefits and paid vacations for the privilege of working 18-hour days, six or seven days a week, for the same or less money. Since you will spend so much time at it, make sure you love whatever business you are getting into and that it makes sense for you to be in that business.

Laundries were a great business, but I was starting to get burned out. So we sold the stores at the right time. We decided it was best to sell while the equipment was still relatively new, the cash flow strong, and we were on top. The older we let the laundries get the more maintenance cost we would have which would eat into profit. Little did we know that six months after selling huge new competition would enter our market, killing our first laundromat. It seems we made the right decision which is the final lesson from my laundromat adventure: Don't let your ego get involved in your business. If you succeed or if you fail, be able to walk away when it makes sense. There is always another deal.

SUCCESS SNAPSHOT

HOUSE CLEANING SERVICES

"You Don't Need Money Or An Education To Start"

INCOME RANGE: $18 - $35/hour or more.

TRAINING REQUIRED: None but ability to clean.

START-UP COSTS: Less than $1,000.

PHYSICAL REQUIREMENTS: must be able to vacuum, move furniture, stoop to clean floors and toilets, kneel, and lift.

SPECIAL SKILLS: Common sense, enjoy cleaning and organizing, and have an attention to detail.

NEED TO INCORPORATE: No, but in this industry having insurance and even being bonded is a great selling feature. It is very inexpensive, only a few hundred dollars per year.

THINGS TO READ TO HELP YOU: *Speed Cleaning 101: Cut Your Cleaning Time in Half!* **by Laura Dellutri** lauradellutri.com.

House cleaning services is a great business opportunity if you like making decent money, like cleaning, and you don't mind flexible hours or working alone. Whether a house, an apartment, or an office, everyone has a need for regular cleaning. As our lives become more hectic, more and more people are turning to house cleaners for help. Housecleaning is not a field just for women. Many men love the great money and steady year-round work this industry provides.

House cleaning services is different than janitorial services, mostly due to the size and focus of the business and the number of employees each has. You can easily start a house cleaning service by yourself and add employees if you want or even grow the housekeeping service into a full blown janitorial service like "Sherry" did. House cleaning services can be started for under $1,000, but janitorial companies are larger businesses often requiring $50,000 or more to start.

The average house cleaner has weekly, bi-weekly, or monthly accounts, taking anywhere from one to four hours to clean. When a house cleaner submits a cleaning bid they should review the services the client wants and how frequently. Ask if there are any unique items that require special care, like hardwood floors, marble floors, granite tops, mirrors, pet areas, or kid's areas, etc. Vacuuming and floors, cleaning bathrooms, entrance doors, and kitchens are normal in any basic clean. Dusting can be performed monthly whereas cleaning vents, light fixtures and ceiling fans are often done quarterly. Some clients want the cleaner to do laundry, fold clothes, and often will ask for a special cleaning, like a barbeque grill, garage sweep, or a refrigerator defrost and cleaning. A good cleaner--one that earns referrals--will be available for special projects at the client's request.

If at all possible, both you and the customer will be much happier if you can get the customer to agree to allow you to do a special deep clean to start. This gets the house up to a condition where it can be easily maintained with normal cleaning sessions. Both you and your customer will be amazed how much of a difference a professional deep clean will make. In a deep clean you work from top to bottom, cleaning everything. Do things the customer normally wouldn't do for themselves, like vacuuming under couch seat cushions, vents, and moving furniture. If they can't afford a deep clean, which is usually twice the normal cleaning rate (for twice the work) then leave time in your bid so that 15 - 30 minutes of each clean can be devoted to deep cleaning. With each cleaning session work your way around so that after a few times you have given a deep clean to all of the property.

When you first bid the job you should agree in advance on the hourly rate or what the cost per clean is. To be the most professional, submit your bid proposal in writing, typed if you can. A sample bid proposal is located in Section 3 of this book, and on the website illegaltolegal.org. Before starting the cleaning job have the customer sign two originals of the bid proposal, giving one to them and keeping one for you. There are many bid templates available online and at local and online printers.

What is necessary in the bid proposal is to have a detail of the scope of work, the rate, the time projected, a statement of who is paying for chemicals/trash bags, and terms for payment. Also agree up front how any pets will be dealt with during the clean, and if they will give you keys to the home, let you in, or leave the house unlocked for you to clean. Have them show you where all the trash cans are and where they want you to empty trash.

In my opinion, under normal circumstances you shouldn't allow the homeowner to be present while you clean as they often look over your shoulder and can be a source of frustration while you are trying to serve them. They are helpful to have there for the first clean to show you around and help you become familiar with their home.

I paid my cleaner $320/month to clean my house weekly in a four-hour block of time. That worked out to be $20 per hour. I paid for the cleaning supplies my cleaner used on my home. Each visit he swept, mopped, and vacuumed; dusted; cleaned the glass on my entry and patio doors; swept the garage and entrance porch; cleaned the toilets, sinks, and showers in each bathroom; cleaned all mirrors; emptied all trash cans; cleaned each kitchen and wet bar in my home; cleaned the outside grill, and made sure all furniture was arranged in place. He also put leather lotion on the furniture monthly.

What a deal for four hours of pay! Who wants to clean on their day off? I didn't. What he did in four hours would take me all day, plus he cleaned more things than I and cleaned better than I. There was no greater feeling than coming home to a house being in order, smelling clean, with me knowing I didn't have to do it. My home became a sanctuary I could enjoy. There are a lot of people just like me who will be thrilled to find a conscientious, dependable, honest, professional cleaner like you to give their money to.

Special cleaning is a great source of extra money. You could clean up before or after a party, or before or after your client has houseguests. Everyone needs help spring cleaning. Work with a realtor and specialize in doing deep cleans for people about to put their homes on the market.

Make sure you let your client know what hourly rate applies to special cleaning projects as well, if they schedule the special clean in advance during your normal clean. If the special clean requires a special trip, charge a $35 or more trip charge if the special cleaning project takes less than two hours to perform. Of course you can create customer goodwill and encourage special cleaning projects if you let them know that you might waive the normal trip charge as a customer bonus. If you do that let them know you appreciate referrals for your work.

If you can, try to get cleaning clients in the same neighborhoods or buildings as your current clients. On the same trip you can service two or three customers, making more money and saving on driving time and expense. A great way to get referrals is to waive the trip fee, or give free special cleaning for clients that refer new customers. Try offering a free deep clean if they refer four new customers.

Getting started:
Buy your cleaning supplies in concentrated form if you can. Check out your local janitorial supply store. For instance, I can buy a quart bottle of concentrated window cleaner for $19 that makes over 100 gallons of professional grade glass cleaner. That's far cheaper than the best price of glass cleaner in bulk at Costco, Sam's Club, or Walmart, and, it's a different product than what the customer normally buys.

To get started, at a minimum you will want:

1. Four to six professional quality spray bottles. Don't get the cheap ones! Buy a good quality one that will always perform. The amount of time you save with good equipment will more than pay for the higher cost quickly. Always keep them filled before you go to your job, and have back-ups ready and with you, hence my recommendation for so many of them.
2. Concentrated glass cleaner to make your own glass cleaner.
3. Concentrated neutral cleaner. This is your general go-to work horse cleaner than you will use on most surfaces.
4. An "orange cleaner" product, for tough items, sinks, and toilets.
5. Oven cleaner.
6. Toilet bowl cleaner and brush.
7. A good vacuum cleaner, specifically a back-mounted one if you can afford it. They work great, are light weight, and pay for themselves quickly with the amount of time they save you. Get one that doesn't require bags which will save you money in the long run.
8. A box of good cleaning rags that you can wash and reuse which is cheaper than using mostly paper towels.
9. Febreeze, or another deodorizer.
10. Bleach.
11. Pine Sol.
12. Carpet cleaner, and spot remover.

13. Stain remover, and a "stain stick."
14. A good dust mop (for hard surface flooring) Try a micro fiber pad that is washable.
15. A good broom and dust pan, plus a Swiffer type broom and mop.
16. A dust wand for dusting.
17. An extension pole for the dust wand.
18. Scrub brushes, scraper, and (2) toothbrushes.
19. 1- and 2-gallon buckets.
20. A single-step lightweight step stool, for cleaning mirrors and wiping on top of refrigerators.
21. A lightweight aluminum step ladder, like a 4' ladder if available. This will help you get to light fixtures and ceiling fans, and you can use it to change light bulbs for the client if needed.
22. A professional janitor's mop bucket, mop, and several mop heads.
23. Floor shine, based on the type(s) of floors a client has.
24. Micro fiber towels: great for general cleaning, windows, and mirrors.
25. Some good quality paper towels.
26. Good quality trash bags, in various sizes like waste-basket size, kitchen trash can size, and yard/leaf bags.
27. Pumice stone for water stains on porcelain.
28. Granite and stone cleaner.
29. Any special product your customer may require for their clean, and ask if they have any product preferences.
30. A carry bin to organize and carry your cleaning products.

If you shop right and watch your pennies you should be able to get all of this for under $600. Check Craigslist for the backpack vacuum as well.

Potential customers:
1. Current customers of dissatisfied cleaners (your best bet!).
2. Homeowners and renters (houses, apartments, condos, and townhomes); managers and executives; single adults; busy families with kids; and empty nesters enjoying life.
3. Shared rentals. People that share a rental with roommates often argue about each roommate doing their part cleaning, but if they each would chip in their share of the cleaning, most cleaning-related arguments would cease.
4. Move-out cleans for landlords and property management companies needing to clean rental units after the previous tenant moves.

5. Contractors and homebuilders needing a detail construction clean-up after they finish a project but before they turn it over to their customers.
6. Small offices and businesses.
7. Bars and restaurants.
8. Theaters, churches *and much more.*
9. Anyone desiring a sanitary environment.

For tips on cleaning, pick up *Speed Cleaning 101 – Cut Your Cleaning Time in Half* by Laura Dellutri published by Meredith Publishing. She teaches practical proven methods for speed cleaning which will make you more money. There are also articles on cleaning tips that you can access by clicking on the "cleaning" tab along the bottom of her website lauradellutri.com. Please note: my reference to her book and website do not imply any endorsement or collaboration with or from Laura Dellutri.

Let me share "Sherry's" inspiring story of how she started a house cleaning service, and where it took her.

SHERRY'S STORY:
I am so proud of "Sherry." After her children were born, her family was in need of extra income, and she started her own daycare from her home. As her kids grew, Sherry wanted a business that would get her out of the house and help her earn more money. Without a college degree, the only jobs she could qualify for wouldn't even cover the cost of daycare. Then Sherry was inspired: she could clean homes figuring she could make money doing something she did anyway.

She looked at ads for house cleaners and soon realized they were making great money and could set their own hours. With no assistance or training, but after plenty of research, Sherry placed an ad promoting her new venture. Little did she know her new career was born and to what heights of success it would take her.

After a few years of successful house cleaning Sherry started to help other people get into the business, for free at first. Soon demand for her knowledge and help became so great she started charging for it. From there she started a cleaning referral service from which she fed business to the house cleaners she helped start. Soon that referral service started generating leads for large accounts.

By this time Sherry hired cleaning employees and her janitorial company was formed. Her janitorial company grew into offices in two cities with around 100 employees and substantial annual sales. She later sold her company for a handsome profit.

Only in America can vision and hard work take you from the bathroom to the boardroom. If she launched a successful career from nothing, you can too!

SUCCESS SNAPSHOT

JANITORIAL SERVICES

"Clean Up By Cleaning Up"

INCOME RANGE: $50,000 - $250,000 or more per year.

TRAINING REQUIRED: none but expertise in commercial cleaning methods.

START UP COSTS: At least $50,000 or more. Payroll is your largest expense and you must have at least two or three months of payroll expenses in the bank. This is necessary since some commercial accounts take 30, 60, or 90 days to pay, and you will need money to pay your people if you want to keep operating until your receivables catch up. "Receivables" is more banker and accountant lingo that means "money you expect to collect from business you already performed." Other than payroll, count on about $1,500/crew member start-up costs. You will need even more funds if you provide a company mini-van or vehicle. The need for that can be avoided if the staff work at only one location, or if you can pay them mileage or reimburse their gas to use their car to travel between work locations.

SPECIAL SKILLS: Hiring, managing, and keeping a crew of cleaners; ability to do business-to-business marketing and sales; knowledge of commercial floor care.

NEED TO INCORPORATE: No, but advisable for liability and credibility.

INSURANCE NEEDS: You will definitely need liability insurance for your business, insurance for any work vehicle, you should be bonded (a great selling point, and not expensive at all) and you will need worker's compensation coverage.

FRANCHISES: There are franchises available but before investing with any franchise, interview franchisees to see if they feel the investment was worth it and if they feel they get adequate support and training from the franchisor. Ask yourself if you can do the same business as well or better than the franchise, then decide if the franchise is worth the investment.

OFFICE SPACE: You will need office space to operate. Try to rent space in a building that will barter rent with your cleaning.

The janitorial services industry has great potential: every building needs to be cleaned. Small- to medium-sized businesses are traditionally your best target. Larger companies are becoming great prospects as well, as employers wrestle with nationalized healthcare, more and more companies will look to sub-contract out tasks they used to perform in-house.

Janitorial services differs from house cleaning services in these ways:

1. Janitorial services are more complex than just house cleaning as the properties being cleaned are usually larger.

2. There are usually more employees working for the janitorial company.

3. Many people have grown into janitorial services from house cleaning.

4. Your profit margins aren't as great with janitorial services due to higher overhead but you are doing greater volume.

5. You need more cash reserves for janitorial services, so you can cover your payroll while you wait for your customers to pay you.

6. The most difficult part of a janitorial company is constantly hiring and training workers. Turnover is high in this industry but if you take good care of your workers and treat them with respect your turnover can be much less. Still, managing staff and all the moving parts of cleaning multiple locations are the hardest and most stressful aspects of operating a janitorial service.

7. House cleaners mostly work in the daytime and early evening whereas janitorial companies usually work after-hours or overnight. You as the owner/operator can be called at night for staff "no-shows" or to handle problems that occur. Even if you don't work with the crews, you should periodically inspect their work. John Maxwell calls this "management by walking around." Your team will take pride in their job if they see you frequently, and know that you care about them and their work.

8. A janitorial company requires more equipment than house cleaning. In addition to everything that a house cleaner uses, you may need these extra items for each work crew and/or each job location:

   a. A work cart that holds a 40 - 55 gallon plastic trash can. The cart should have bins, hooks, and cubbies for all of the worker's tools and supplies they will use, except the vacuum.

   b. Any special cleaning supplies or tools that each specific job may require.

   c. Carpet cleaning equipment, tools, and materials to spot clean stained carpeting.

   d. Squeegees, mop buckets, and mop heads for stripping, cleaning, and waxing the floors.

   e. Your company should have at least one floor buffer with pads and chemicals to allow you to care for hard surface flooring. You could even make a janitorial company that specializes just in floor care and make good money.

Janitorial services can be performed daily, Monday-Wednesday-Friday, or weekly. They can be full-service, where you provide all the cleaning supplies and trash can liners, or they can provide the supplies for you. Most contracts seem to be full-service and include emptying all trash cans each time you clean.

Janitorial Services can bill the following ways:

1. Charge by the square foot of space cleaned. Take the square footage and multiply it by what you charge per square foot and then divide by twelve to get the monthly cost. If you're bidding a contract, ask what they were paying, and what they are willing to pay, to determine if their business is worth pursuing.

2. Charge by the week, or the month.

3. You can charge by the hour, but I don't advise this method because eventually every business owner will think they can replace you with a cheap in-house cleaner to save money. They don't consider the hassle they will have staffing and supervising a cleaner and what happens if that worker doesn't show up.

Promote janitorial services like you would promote a lawn service or snow removal service by farming and marketing to real estate companies, property management companies, shopping centers, and to the owners of restaurants, bars, convenience stores, drug stores, grocery stores, office buildings, and more.

If you want to buy an existing janitorial business they generally sell for a price equal to one year's gross income. In business lingo the ratio of the gross income of the business to selling price of a business is called the "multiple" or the "purchase price multiple." Before you buy any business, make sure you know what the standard multiple is in that industry so you are not overpaying and so you can tell if you are getting a good deal or not. Laundries and restaurants typically sell for one year's gross income while there are some businesses that sell for as much as three to ten times the annual gross income.

For instance, lawn services contracts (not including equipment) generally sell for a multiple equal to three months of gross income. Ben got a great deal buying the troubled lawn service when he bought the contracts plus all the vehicles, trailers, and equipment, for three months' of gross income.

One reason to report all of your income is to increase the value of your business. This helps you when you need to borrow money or sell your business like Sherry did when she sold her janitorial company.

You can use a business broker to buy or sell a business, but beware: many business brokers are not licensed and may not use the best trade practices. Never buy a business based on potential income, "proforma" income or estimated potential income. Insist on seeing actual books for the last three to five years with bank statements and tax returns. Sign a confidentiality agreement. If they do not give you this information, then walk away.

If you feel pressured to complete a business deal you should walk away from it. There is always another business to buy or another contract to bid without drama or pressure. If the purchase price is too high or the terms not to your benefit, realize it's probably easier for you to start your own business then to live with the regret of a less-than-perfect deal.

It worked great for Sherry: it might work great for you, too!

SUCCESS SNAPSHOT

PERSONAL TRAINER

"You Are A Walking Billboard"

INCOME RANGE: $25-$250/hour or more.

TRAINING: Years of gym use, plus studying for certification.

LICENSING: Varies by state, but most insurance companies require you to be licensed in order to get insured. Most gyms require ongoing proof of insurance for you to train there. There are a lot of different training programs to get licensed with, from online to university level. Check with your state to see what is required in your area, what fits your budget, and what training/licensing can help you reach the type of clients you want to serve. If you can pass a ninth grade biology class you can easily pass the certification test.

SPECIAL SKILLS: You have to be a great manager of time, be likable, have an outgoing personality, have the ability to read people, be a good conversationalist, be able to motivate people, and have the ability to work with lots of personality types and backgrounds. Knowledge of muscle groups, nutrition, and anatomy is very helpful.

EXPERIENCE: None required, but your body is your billboard, so you should know your way around a gym.

THINGS TO READ: To get licensed study the coursework and find books and articles to help you study basic anatomy in plain language. I also suggest the book *Body For Life* and reputable fitness magazines that serve your target market.

NEED TO INCORPORATE: No

Do you like to exercise? Are you in good shape? Do you find yourself giving workout tips to people in the gym? Do you like helping people succeed? Personal training might be a perfect business for you.

There's more to personal training than just working out. A personal trainer has to be as or more disciplined with their time as they are with their bodies. Personal training requires you to convert your time into dollars because you bill by the hour.

A personal trainer has to know more than just how to lift weights. They have to know how to teach others to exercise and achieve their desired results. That requires being able to recognize people's body types, how to motivate them, and how far you can push them. Every client has different goals and personalities, therefore you can't deal with everyone the same way. You must be able to adapt to their needs and personality type. Remember, they are paying your bills and putting food on your table.

Is personal training a good business to get into? Exercise makes you feel better, improve your appearance, have more energy, and it improves your quality of life and health. Who do you know that doesn't want a better life? Our country is becoming increasingly obese and unhealthy. More than sixty-five percent of the population is overweight or obese. This negatively affects almost 200,000,000 people. That's a *HUGE* potential market, pun intended! This is a problem that you can make money solving if you are passionate about it and approach it properly.

There are many ways to make money as a personal trainer. A few include:

1. Being an employee or independent contractor at a gym. A lot of gyms offer personal training, but don't want to mess with the hassle of having employees. So they use independent contractors and split the fees. Contact gyms in your area to see if this is an option for you.

2. Renting gym access for you to train your clients. This is usually at smaller fitness centers, warehouse gyms, or private health clubs. This is great for all since the gym where you train gets your rent money and they often attract your clients as new members.

3. Running boot camp group classes, body pump classes, Zumba classes, etc. Let's say you charged $40 for an hour Body Pump class, with six students. You just earned $240/hour! These can be at a gym, a senior center, hospital, or a park. The sky is the limit!

4. Doing corporate wellness programs and classes for corporations and groups.

5. Hiring other trainers as sub-contractors or employees.

6. Starting your own fitness studio, gym, or health club.

7. Doing in-home personal training like my friend Nick.

NICK'S STORY:

In the early 2000s Nick was an 18 year-old college student who was athletic, had an outgoing personality, was entrepreneurial, and was sick of working the low paying jobs that fit into his school schedule. He paid $900 for a week-long course to earn a personal training certification. Once licensed, he went to work for a large national health club chain.

Nick's job, in addition to personal training, was to attract and sell personal training to new clients. Nick got his start just visiting with people in the gym while they worked out. His friendliness, knowledge, and the condition of his body all helped Nick strike up conversations and friendships with the members. He then would offer a free initial training session and fitness evaluation, and used the success of that free session to sign up new training clients.

Nick noticed it seemed that the big gyms wanted the customer dependent on them for life instead of teaching them lifestyle changes so they wouldn't need a trainer someday. Nick realized when he showed clients how to make positive lifestyle changes that they would refer all their friends and family to him.

Nick, due to his passion for fitness and helping people, quickly became the most popular trainer at that large gym. They paid him $12/hour while he was personal training, $8/hour when he wasn't training. The health club was charging Nick's clients $70/hour and Nick quickly saw an opportunity to help his clients save money and make a lot more money than he was making working at the gym. When Nick launched on his own he worked part-time--about fifteen hours per week--and earned $35,000/year doing something he loved! He was on track to make $100,000/year but he used personal training to launch into something bigger in life.

Because of a potential conflict of interest with his employer, Nick trained his private clients off-site. It made sense for Nick to target clients with workout equipment at home or that had in-home gyms. He later even focused on and "farmed" specific upper income areas where he had customers or where well-off middle aged professionals lived. Nick went door-to-door, introducing himself. He left a card or flyer that explained his in-home training services. This is another example of a successful entrepreneur who knew that "all marketing is personal." Nick also used Google AdWords and Craigslist to promote his business. He had a website, but said he never got business from his website. Nick said that if he could talk face-to-face with a serious prospect then he likely would have them as a new client.

Nick charged his customers $60-$100/hour, and customized workouts and training for their needs. Most of his customers were housewives. Often after feeling the benefits of training the wife would convince the husband to train as well. Nick would give discounts for couples who trained. His clients trusted Nick as he kept relations strictly professional, which was important to the husbands of the wealthy wives he trained. Because of client trust, Nick regularly got referrals from his customers.

Here are some tips from Nick to help you build a solid personal training business:

1. You are paid to be cheerful, positive, helpful, and in a good mood: even if you're not. Give people a reason to want to spend their time and money with you.

2. Stress your worth to them. Let them know you are there to help them reach their goals, not to make them dependent on you. In a bad economy the first thing to go is usually the Trainer so make yourself valuable to them by helping them achieve their goals.

3. Be a great listener and be able to sincerely have great conversations. How can you know what their goals are, and if they are happy their progress, unless you listen to them and engage them?

4. Find out why they want a trainer. This may sound obvious, but not everyone uses a trainer for the same reason. Some people want paid motivation. Others want someone to push them harder than they would push themselves. Some want a workout buddy or friend. Knowing why they want a trainer goes a long way to developing a loyal client relationship. You make more money, and get more referrals, from continuing to train happy customers than you do by finding new customers to replace lost ones.

5. Be open to the unexpected. Nick trained a lady who was so impressed with their sessions that she convinced her husband to start training also. Nick trained them three times per week, an hour each, for $50/hour. One day the husband let Nick know he wanted a daily early morning jogging partner. Nick quickly agreed to jog with him at no additional charge. Why didn't Nick charge him? He was already getting $1,200/month from this customer. That customer then became a great source of referrals.

6. Make your customers pay a week or a month in advance and let them know they have to cancel/reschedule missed sessions twenty-four hours in advance. People will miss sessions and having them pay in advance will help motivate them to attend. Otherwise if you let them miss sessions without penalty you'll end up broke and bored without training sessions. Services like Square make credit card and debit card processing convenient, portable, and affordable for you.

7. Keep your schedule organized. Nothing will kill your reputation and your business like missing appointments, double booking, and being late. I used to have a tendency to run late until my biggest client told me after once making him wait ten minutes that "punctuality is the beginning of credibility." I made over $1.7 million cash in my pocket doing business with this client over the years. I didn't make him wait again.

8. If you go to start a fitness studio or gym make sure you have a cushion of at least $15,000 or more available to you in cash or from a loan or line of credit. This cushion will help you through the adjustment period as you get used to the extra expenses in your own facility.

9. Get to know your clients. You will get to know every inch of their bodies, what they can tolerate, the look on their face when they have reached their limit, and whether they have any more push in them or not.

10. Nick observed that "it seems the average client relationship is about three months, which is the same of length of time it takes for most people to see results from training."

11. Don't give up, even when you get a lot of "no's" from people, and always market yourself.

Personal training can be a great part-time income, a lucrative career, or it can help you grow into your own fitness studio, gym, or health club.

"Remember, you are a walking billboard."

-Nick B.

SUCCESS SNAPSHOT

WAREHOUSE GYM / HEALTH CLUB

"People Will Pay For The Best"

"What Is My Target Market, And Why?"

"Vision Is Critical For Success"

START-UP COSTS:

Warehouse Gym: $15,000 - $50,000 depending on the size of space, finishes, and type of equipment. For instance, if you focus on free weights, the cost is much cheaper than if you focus on providing a lot of cardio equipment.

Fitness Studio/Training Studio/Yoga studio: $5,000 - $35,000, also depending on size of space, finishes, and your equipment.

Small Health Club (like 2,500 SF - 5,000 SF) such as a Snap Fitness or an Anytime Fitness: $250,000 - $400,000.

Full Service Health Club over 5,000 SF: $500,000 - $2.5 Million or more.

Do you work out or exercise? I bet if you don't you know someone who does. According to the International Health, Racquet and Sportsclub Association's (IHRSA) 2012 survey currently over 50.2 million people in the United States belong to a gym or health club. Annual gym memberships in the USA total more than $21.8 billion every year. Even though there are more than 30,500 gyms, the industry is growing. With our aging population and obesity at huge levels, the fitness industry is poised to continue to grow--puns intended! I have always said "I was never out of shape since round is still a shape." Unfortunately "round" isn't the shape most of us health-conscious people want to be in.

Maybe you've always wanted to own a gym, but never knew how to approach it. Depending on the type of gym, you might be surprised how affordable and easy it is do once you have a vision for it. Your "vision" is what you want your business to be. Without a vision and planning you will fail. Your vision drives the type of gym you offer, the area you locate it, and the target customers you attract. Start with the end in mind.

For your vision to succeed you need to determine if a need exists for the type of gym you want to provide, who your customers will be, and how you will be able to connect your future customers to your business. Make sure you read the Success Snapshot on a Martial Arts Studio since it gives great guidance on doing a market study and selecting a location. Let's start here with the types of gyms you could operate.

A "warehouse gym" is the newest fitness craze. They usually are smaller ranging from 1,500 SF - 3,000 SF without much cardio equipment. These focus on free weights and functional equipment. Functional training uses things like tractor tires, ropes, kettle bells, bands, pull-up bars, and things that make you use natural body movements. This is growing in popularity in the fitness and training worlds. Customers like warehouse gyms because usually only serious exercisers use them and they aren't as packed and intimidating as some of the larger health clubs. Warehouse gyms usually aren't fancy and are in well-located industrial buildings with minimal finishes and facilities. Often they are without showers but with men's and women's changing rooms and restrooms.

A lot of independent personal trainers will rent monthly or weekly access to warehouse gyms to train their clients. This is a great way for a warehouse gym owner to add extra income, offer training without having employees, and get new members from the trainers' clients who join the warehouse gym to workout at.

Fitness or training studios usually focus on group classes like Crossfit, boot camps, body pump, Zumba, yoga, martial arts, and personal training. These may or may not have weights or other workout equipment in them. Most will have changing rooms, gymnastic mats, one or more mirrored classrooms with sound systems and extra bands, bars, weights, dumbbells, jump boxes, and other things equipped for class settings of 10-20 people. This type of gym focuses on group classes and personal training for revenue.

There is the traditional health club or gym which can be smaller or a larger, fancy or basic, expensive or simple. These usually focus on selling large amounts of memberships. In fact, they typically try to _way_ oversell memberships, knowing that only a small percentage of members will ever use the facilities at one time. Personal training is a secondary source of income and usually is done by an employee of the health club and not an independent personal trainer.

All gyms, health clubs, and fitness studios provide a service and make extra money selling health supplements (like protein powders and bars), and vending (like bottled water and protein shakes) and sometimes equipment (like weight lifting gloves, yoga mats, etc.). Some even sell fruit, healthy snacks, and chicken breast sandwiches.

There are two basic kinds of health clubs: the smaller ones (2,500 - 5,000 SF) or the larger ones which are over 5,000 SF and can be 80,000 - 100,000 + SF. Smaller clubs such as an Anytime Fitness franchise can be operated with minimal staff while larger health clubs require more employees, more space, more equipment, and more overhead. I like to advise you to start small unless you can afford a bigger investment and your market dictates a bigger club.

To get in the business you could buy a gym if you can find one for sale or start your own. If you start your own, where do you begin? Think about your strengths, weaknesses, and passions as they relate to the health club industry. How do they relate to your target customer? If you fire a shotgun it usually sprays everywhere except your target. If you fire a rifle you are more likely to hit your target because you can aim. Your target customer is who you are aiming to serve. Is your passion and your skill in personal training? If so, you may want to start a warehouse gym or a fitness studio that focuses on training for your target customers. Are you a serious power-lifter and you want to make a specialized power-lifting gym? Are you in an affluent area with a lot of retirees that need a high quality health club that caters to their physical and social needs? What requirements does your city have for gyms?

Where do you want to locate your new gym? Get the map out and mark all of your competitor's locations on the map and see if the map reveals any obvious areas that aren't being served. Sometimes areas not being served aren't served for a reason, which may be a sign to stay away. Other times the un-served or underserved areas are in growth areas. A gym just hasn't located there yet. That could be a good opportunity for you. Maybe there are one or more successful large gyms in the area you want to locate, and you want to do a specialized studio close by. That could be a great opportunity as well, as long as what you do is different from and better than your competition. Notice I didn't say "cheaper than you competition." Your work has value and I think you are always better off charging more and being the best at what you do. People will pay for the best.

Let me share the story of my friend Chris with you. He was a personal trainer who then was able to become a partner in a new warehouse gym.

CHRIS' STORY:
Chris was a hard working college student who loved lifting weights, golfing, and being outdoors. His job was lawn mowing at a golf course, which allowed us to golf free when he was off work. He was studying landscaping to be a grounds superintendent at a golf course, and he wanted to own his own lawn service. But he spent so much time at the gym, someone suggested he take classes and become a personal trainer. It made sense that he could earn a lot more than he did at the golf course. He was at the gym a lot anyway. While working out, people would always ask his advice because he was in great shape and was personable. That was an example of him being "a walking billboard." Chris was a quiet, patient person who loved helping others so becoming a personal trainer was a natural for him.

After he got his personal training license he worked for a national health club. Like my friend Nick, he hated the high-pressure sales tactics his employer tried to force him to use. There was a fancy new independent health club opening up in town, so Chris and other trainers flocked there to be part of one of the newest and best facilities in town.

The fancy new gym had a lot of nice features such as expensive finishes and furnishings, all new weights and cardio machines, a rockin' snack and juice bar, plus nice locker rooms and classrooms. The physical amenities were tremendous. After working there a short while Chris realized something important. Having the fanciest newest gym means nothing if the business is disorganized. Having a good system is the difference between success and failure. For all their faults, the big nationals did have a much better system. That's part of why they were successful. Many people buy franchises to get a good system. Of course, not all franchises are good businesses, and some are much better than others at giving you training in a system to make you successful. Why is a good system important? Isn't it good enough that I work hard and offer a great product or great service?

Robert Kiyosaki in his best-selling book *Rich Dad, Poor Dad* asks this question: since McDonald's doesn't have the best hamburgers money can buy, how can they be the phenomenal success they are? It's not the marketing, product line, slogan, price, or even location that made McDonald's the global powerhouse it is. McDonald's is the leader because they have the best system. A system will take you to success faster than "winging it," even if you aren't trying to open more than 25,000 locations worldwide.

You don't have to buy an expensive franchise to have a good system. Working for a successful business in your field is a good way to learn your future competitor's system. You can probably find ways to improve or change it. That's what Chris and his business partner Dave did. Having a good system isn't about writing a thick operations manual, it's about caring enough about your business and your reputation to make sure you create and maintain a consistent product and service that you're proud to put your name on. Inconsistency was killing the new fancy gym where Chris and Dave worked. They were losing employees and customers. Chris knew he didn't want to go back to the big national gym. After seeing what his employers earned on his training ($50-$80/hour), and what he made as an employee, he thought he could do much better opening a small gym that provided what he knew the customers wanted.

Since warehouse gyms are growing in popularity they knew they wanted to open one that focused on personal training. Chris and Dave wanted their new warehouse gym to provide a peaceful well-organized environment where clients could come in, work out, and get on with their day. They wouldn't use high pressure sales tactics. They have made themselves unique by offering a membership with no initiation fees and a monthly contract that can be cancelled anytime.

They leased a small 2,000 SF bay and equipped their facility with $20,000 of nice, used equipment to start. They had a loyal following of clients from their old jobs that followed them, as well as a lot of trainers who were former coworkers who wanted a place to independently train. Chris and Dave did something brilliant that helped them be profitable from the beginning. They leased weekly access to independent trainers to train from their gym. The trainers paid $100/week and their clients could use the gym free while they were being trained. Clients paid their trainers directly. The independent trainers loved it because one or two sessions would pay the rent and they wouldn't have to be under the thumb of a large gym. They could also make more money. The trainers averaged twenty sessions per week. Chris and Dave signed up enough independent trainers to pay the rent on the facility. Many of the trainer's clients joined their gym and word of mouth from satisfied customers made their business grow quickly. This was a win-win situation for all.

Chris and Dave regularly promoted their business through their Facebook page, and they encouraged their clients to write favorable reviews on Yahoo, Google, and Angie's List. In their first year of business they won the award for "Best Personal Training Gym in the City" and they haven't looked back since.

They weren't the cheapest, but they worked hard to be the best at their little niche in the market.

Find something unique, do it better than anyone else, and don't be afraid to charge for it!

> *"People will pay for the best."*

SUCCESS SNAPSHOT

U-HAUL DEALER

"Create Something From Nothing"

INCOME: $75k - $150k or more.

START-UP COSTS: From $0 to $1,000.

WHAT NEEDED TO START: A top location with an existing retail business and room to park trucks and trailers. For more details see uhaul.com/dealer.

EXPERIENCE NEEDED: None other than general business experience.

TRAINING REQUIRED: Classes online with U-Haul University, plus two days of testing for competency and quality assurance.

SPECIAL SKILLS NEEDED: Ability to give excellent customer service, while multi-tasking, and possessing the ability to say "no." Light mechanical skills are helpful also.

Think about how many times in your life you've moved. Do you remember how many times you rented a truck or trailer? Which company comes to mind first when you think about renting a truck or trailer?

U-Haul is one of America's best-known and best-loved brands. A well-run, well-located U-Haul operation is a very profitable enterprise. How profitable? You earn 20-30 percent of the rentals you process, most of which come from U-Haul corporate through their website, plus your own walk-in neighborhood business. You get to keep all the profits from selling moving supplies. Sometimes you see an established dealership for sale for $150,000 + but did you know you can start one *for free*?

For most people, being a U-Haul dealer is a great addition to their main business, but my friend Will made the U-Haul dealership his main business. To become a U-Haul dealer you must have an established business to operate from, but you don't have to own that business.

What other national franchise is free? None that I am aware of, and certainly none with the success, credibility, and national network like U-Haul has.

WILL'S STORY

My friend Will was a U-Haul employee, manager, and trainer for fifteen years earning $75,000 per year. He knew their system inside and out and literally trained hundreds of business owners to operate a successful U-Haul dealership. After years of helping everyone else make big money Will decided to venture out on his own and he opened his first U-Haul location as an independent dealer. U-Haul provided the trucks, trailers, training, signage, and computer programs for free. Will provided the location, computer, printer, phone lines, and labor. He started his U-Haul dealership for well under $1,000.

This Success Snapshot is based entirely on what Will told me, and is not officially sanctioned by U-Haul. Check uhaul.com/dealer for more on how to become a U-Haul dealer should this exciting opportunity interest you.

How much money did Will make in his first year? Before I answer that, let me ask you this: if you were earning a $75,000/year paycheck how much money would you need to earn to walk away from that and take the risk of starting your own business? In Will's first year, with his first location and doing moving services he cleared $140,000, and Will didn't even own the location where he put his dealership. Now Will has plans to open multiple locations in his market using the same strategy I describe below.

How did Will do it? Will checked his market for a potential location that was on a high-traffic street and was more than a mile from the next closest U-Haul. He looked for sites that had room on their lot for trucks and trailers and was in an area that would do good business as a U-Haul dealer. A good business area was one where people would perform their own moves, was growing, or were moving into the area from out of state.

Will embraced inner city locations because "even people getting evicted who couldn't pay their rent would always come up with the money to rent a U-Haul so they can keep their stuff," he told me. Will loved putting stores in the inner-city. He said they always were great money makers if run professionally and with good service. Most inner-city areas are underserved for goods and services anyway, and Will ran his U-Haul dealership as a good neighborhood business.

Will had a location in mind. He had approached the owner of this independent gas station if he would become a U-Haul dealer. The gas station owner at first declined, saying he was too busy running his gas station. When Will decided to go on his own he then approached this same gas station owner and said "Can I operate my own U-Haul dealership from here and pay you a cut of the action?" That business owner said yes. Not only did he get his share of the trailer rental but the U-Haul rental was great for his gas station business as nearly every customer returning a truck or trailer gassed up at his gas station and bought other things as well.

Do you know of any places that _you_ could do the same thing Will did, and get yourself into the U-Haul business for free? Please see the next Success Snapshot "Mover" for Will's entire story.

"Create something from nothing"

SUCCESS SNAPSHOT

MOVER

*"Don't wait for perfect conditions, but figure out how
to make your business happen with what you have."*

*"Listen to your customers: they'll let you need what they need.
Make money serving their needs."*

INCOME: $500 - $1,000/day or more.

EQUIPMENT NEEDED: Access to moving trucks which can be rented
as needed. Acquire moving pads and blankets, boxes, moving supplies,
bins, professional appliance dollies, two - wheel carts, and moving sleds.

START-UP COSTS: Under $1,000, if you rent equipment. $35,000 -
$50,000 if you buy or lease trucks to start. The most important money
you can spend is on insurance, advertising, business cards, and flyers: in
that order.

TRAINING NEEDED: None except the ability to pack and move with
care.

NEED TO INCORPORATE: Helpful as soon as you can afford it.

MOVER: WILL'S STORY, continued

Remember my friend Will who was great at making something out of
nothing and started the successful U-Haul dealership with virtually no
money? While operating his U-Haul dealership Will was often asked by
customers for a referral on a mover. One day a customer was in a bind
and offered Will a lot of money to help them unload the truck the
customer had rented from Will's U-Haul dealership. Will contacted some
friends who needed money and hired them as laborers. Will's moving
company was born on the spot because Will listened to what his
customers wanted. He made money serving their need.

What was brilliant was he had a steady stream of U-Haul customers, many of whom welcomed hiring Will's crew to help them load and unload their goods. When he expanded beyond U-Haul customers Will could rent his own U-Hauls and not have money tied up into acquiring, operating, or maintaining equipment. U-Haul and other rental companies provide their own insurance and maintenance costs on their equipment. When Will rented equipment he made sure he always accepted the "extra insurance option" for added protection for around $15 or so. Often his guys were only hired to help unload his customer's items so sometimes he didn't even have equipment rental costs.

Here's how Will made money: he paid his workers very well, around $15/hour. He used mostly college students, student athletes, even the football players from his local semi-pro football team. The pay he offered, along with occasional bonuses, allowed him to hire high quality movers who were courteous, professional, conscientious, and hard-working. He would bid jobs at a $200 minimum for 2 hours of workers, not counting any rental. He provided two workers that he paid $60 total for their time and cleared $140 gross profit after payroll! After the first two hours it was $100/hour for the crew's time. He charged more if he had to provide a truck or trailer. For larger jobs he could assign multiple crews.

Often customers would ask for extra help beyond just loading or unloading the truck. To give good service Will would help them out. If they went a little over on their time he wouldn't "nickel and dime them." He usually would give up to twenty minutes of grace time without charge. After twenty minutes over he charged the full half hour or hour. Customers would often tip the workers, which was a nice bonus for them. Will made sure the crews received all of their tips.

Will was able to advertise for local moving on short notice and soon branched out from just helping his U-Haul customers to doing conventional moves. Will's next step was to get into out-of-town moves, which were very profitable. At first, his movers helped people load their U-Hauls going out-of-town at the rates quoted above. Your own market may allow you to charge more for providing a moving crew as Will's market was a smaller city with a lot of competition.

Call your competition as a mystery shopper to find out what they charge. When Will started he always was a little below the cost of his competition. He raised his price once he was established. You can even let competition know you are available to help them if they get behind.

Will developed a unique niche for new customers. He contacted local nursing homes and became a preferred mover for their residents by offering them special prices. He charged them full price on their move-ins and half-price on their move-outs. He contacted local colleges and universities to offer special prices for college students moving in and out of the dorms. He farmed upper-income neighborhoods and apartment complexes to distribute flyers with coupons on them for his moving company. Be creative and I'm sure you can think of some gimmick or special service you can offer to get business.

Operationally, Will believes if you are helping to pack a load always have your staff take a photo of the load before it's driven. This helps reduce damage claims. Also it's always best if the customer is driving the rental truck unless you yourself rent it. This further reduces damage claims.

Even if you don't have a U-Haul dealership you can still use Will's example to help you start a moving company. Most movers are booked in advance so provide something they don't: moving on short notice. You can rent trucks or trailers to get you started. Wait to buy your own equipment until you can afford it.

According to Will, the keys to success in business are:
1.   The people. Your team will make or break you. Hire the best, and don't be afraid to pay them accordingly. You get what you pay for. Don't just pay someone a lot of money because he works for you. Tell them the salary, what you expect him to do, and constantly evaluate and make sure they are doing the level of work you want them to do.

2.   Customer Service. You will grow your business faster by going the extra mile and providing exceptional customer service. Make sure your crews are always very careful with customer's belongings. Believe me your customers will notice. Look for little things you can do to show appreciation to the customer and give them a reason to remember you the next time they or their friends need a mover.

3.   Promotion. You must constantly be promoting your business, even when you are busy. Use Google AdWords, Craigslist, and flyers anywhere you can put one up. Make friends with the managers of large apartment complexes, even contact relocation companies and realtor offices to build business. You can offer a referral fee or a discount for realtor's customers, or both.

4.   Don't wait for perfect conditions, but figure out how to make your business happen with what you have at hand. When Will was first asked about movers he wasn't thinking he could be the mover as he didn't have the money to buy moving trucks and set up a moving company. But when he started to think outside of the box, he realized he didn't need money to start a moving company. He made the moving company happen by using what he had at hand: the U-Hauls, which were already insured and maintained. Thus, his moving company was off and running.

Will said he makes $2,000 - $5,000/week from moving, all because he was able to figure out how to fill a customer need with what he had. Don't wait for perfect conditions before you start your business. Figure out how to make what you have work for you, and blast towards your dream of self-employment.

> *"Listen to your customers: they'll let you know what they need. Make money serving their needs."*

SUCCESS SNAPSHOT

FREELANCE GRAPHIC ARTIST

"Give People A Reason To Do Business With You."

"Going The Extra Mile ALWAYS Makes The Difference"

"Always Under-Promise And Over-Perform"

INCOME: $35,000 - $125,000 or more. This could be a great part-time job and a great way to build up the business until you can afford to go full-time. Your income will vary greatly based on whether you are working part-time or full-time, and it will also vary widely based on your type of clients and work you are specializing in.

START-UP COSTS: Little-to-nothing if you already have the computer, software, and access to printers. Your start-up costs can vary widely based on how much equipment you invest in to start, and whether you work from home, an office or a shared office. I always advise people to figure out the bare minimum equipment you need, buy that, and let your business buy more equipment once it has cash flow. Rule #1 of Pelshaw's Principles for Profitable Business is "everything must pay for itself."

EXPERIENCE, TRAINING, & EQUIPMENT REQUIRED: This business requires you to combine artistic talent with business skills. If you are using computer aided graphics proficiency in those programs are needed as well as access to computer programs. Many community colleges, universities, and trade schools offer degrees and certificates in graphic arts, and photography. The best value for your education is the local community college. Most offer night and weekend classes. Certain trade schools charge more for their tuition than some universities, so shop around for your best education value.

Have you ever thought about how important graphic artists are and how often we see their work daily?

Here are but some of what a graphic artist probably designed:
- Every ad, sale flyer, and sign you see, at least the good ones anyway!
- Corporate branding and logos.
- Every product package you use, whether a bag of chips or a detergent box.
- Every page of your favorite catalogue or illustrations in books.
- The cool pages on your favorite websites.
- The covers of the books and magazines you read.
- Cartoons in books, print, magazine, video, and graphics.
- Graphics in videos and presentations.
- Sales floor signage in retail stores.
- Computer and internet icons

I challenge you to go through one day of your life without using something a graphic artist designed or produced. We are visual creatures. Nearly everything we value is visually appealing for one reason or another.

Perhaps you love art or are a talented artist. In this book I tell you the key to success and happiness is to find a business you can own and operate that uses your passions and strengths.

Your passions and strengths will not only get you into your business, make you known and successful, but they will also give you your specialty and your unique proposition or "purple cow." If you love working with kids, you can design products, ads, graphics, or cartoons targeting children. Maybe you're a foodie so menu creation could be your specialty. If you know a lot about cars and car parts working on a catalog for a car parts company could be something good for you to try. You don't need a specialty to start. Take whatever work you can get until you decide what type of work you want to focus on.

Medium- and large-sized companies used to have graphic artist departments in house. Now many of these companies are outsourcing their work to individual graphic artists who work on a project-by-project basis. Find companies that are willing to outsource to you. That's what "Bella" did.

"BELLA'S" STORY:
Before Bella graduated with her degree in graphic arts, she got a part-time job working as a graphic designer in a book store. The pay was low, but it gave her some needed experience. She made a catalog and sales

floor signage for the store. She later quit that job to concentrate on finishing school. After graduation she couldn't find a job so she worked part-time in a ceramics studio for six months where she sharpened her skills as an artist. She then got another part-time job doing graphic arts for a small internet start-up. When Bella started with the internet company she knew nothing about the computers or web pages she was working with, but she's never been afraid to learn or take challenging projects, and grow as a professional in the meantime.

The internet company exposed Bella to the world of creative business. Soon she took side jobs working for companies outsourcing extra work, and those too small to afford their own graphic artist. In the beginning she took whatever work she could find. At first she was trying to survive and pay the bills, but over time the variety of work she did helped to give her a wide range of talent and develop her specialties.

Bella is very friendly, social, and loyal. She got business through networking with friends from school and church to let them know she was available for graphic arts and photography work. After two years at the internet company she built enough business to go out on her own.

Bella does *amazing* work. She did the book cover, the layout, and graphics in this book, plus the logos on our website illegaltolegal.org and my other businesses as well. She's done work on two continents and Bella's work is internationally known as the top of world-class professionalism and creativity. In addition she is a joy to work with.

She's had some tough times, but in eleven years of being self-employed she's never looked back. She loves what she does. She does product packaging, signs, book illustrations, cartoons. One of her passions is creating logos. Logos are a key part of presenting your new business and developing your personal brand. Your logo is your first impression so you should make it count.

If you need a logo for your business Bella can help. You can reach her studios through our website and she and her team can provide you with a custom logo, business card layout, and stationary layout, that you can have printed locally or through an internet printing service. If you want a "turnkey" business start-up package we can get you nearly everything you need to launch your own business. This includes the already mentioned logo, card, and stationary proof for your business, plus federal and state tax identification numbers, incorporation or limited liability company (LLC) papers you can file, and a personalized custom Business Plan Checklist™. You can upgrade your package to a personalized business plan, and even one-on-one business coaching from our expert business coaches if you wish.

According to Bella, here are keys to getting people to do business with you, and success in graphic arts:

1. Doing business as a graphic artist is different than being a graphic artist. You can be the most talented artist in the world but unless you operate professionally and like a real business you cannot make a living being a graphic artist.

2. Many creative people are naturally undisciplined, particularly when it comes to punctuality and deadlines. When you agree to provide a project by a certain date others are depending on you to keep your word. Your reputation and livelihood are on the line so keep your promised deadlines, no matter what.

3. If you are going to miss a deadline, or if you have bad news, be proactive and let your client know quickly when they can expect the project to be completed. They may not like you being late or what you have to say, but they will like your directness, honesty, and communication, even when it's bad news.

4. As a business owner you are selling yourself. You make yourself valuable by doing what you say you are going to do.

5. Always ask for more time for a project than you think you need. Give yourself a little cushion. Creativity is complex and you can never be sure if you will finish a job in thirty minutes or three days. Always under-promise and over-perform and you will get respect and lots of repeat business and referrals.

6. Often it's hard for creative talented people to take constructive criticism. It seems the more talented they are the harder it is for them to take criticism. Don't ever let your ego get in the way of making your client happy. Your client is paying you: you better learn to listen attentively to everything they are telling you about your project and your work, especially if they're not satisfied.

7. Don't take criticism personally. Be thankful they are letting you know their concerns because you wouldn't want to lose a customer over something you could've changed if they had told

you. You have to realize you gain new perspective and grow from the client's criticism. The criticism is not an attack against you or your work but is feedback on how to make the customer happy. You can learn something new from their comments.

8. Sometimes you have to save the client from themselves. For instance, they may have poor ideas or poor taste. You can make suggestions, but never let them feel that their opinions don't matter or that they are inferior to you. Offer the client alternatives and reasons for what you are suggesting. Make it easy for them to agree with you, and don't argue with clients needlessly.

9. Make sure you give them what _they_ want, not necessarily what you want. Your personal tastes may be different than your client's but in the end the customer is paying your bill. Do your work with excellence and in a way that makes them happy to pay your bill in full.

10. Don't be afraid to charge top-dollar for work, but always make the client feel like they are getting a good value for your work. Find a way to go the extra mile, whether it's turning a project in early, giving them extra options, extra proofs, or whatever. Even if it's a little extra work, or extra cost, going the extra mile always pays you rewards. It could be the difference between you and your competition. When you give them extra work, let the customer know what you did and that you aren't charging them for that. Don't go overboard with the extra work, but do enough to where they feel they got a good value and you appreciate them.

11. Because you are charging top dollar, don't "nickel and dime" your clients to death on their bills. Make them feel good about paying you what you charge. That is how you build relationships. Nothing gives you repeat business, and referrals, like building relationships.

12. With new clients, try to get half or a third of the cost of the project up front as a down payment to start. Let your customers know up front your billing terms. Most businesses expect to have thirty days to pay a bill, but some will take sixty or ninety days to pay. Ask them before you bid the job how long it takes them to process payables and what their procedure is to pay bills, like

if they prefer an invoice or a statement. You can offer a two percent discount if they pay the bill within 10 days of getting the bill. In business lingo this is a called a "2%/10" or "2% net 10 days" discount. Your billing terms should be on every invoice or statement you send out.

13. Always treat the client professionally, with kindness and respect, regardless of how they treat you. Don't take abuse from clients. You will have some clients you will have to walk away from, but most will treat you with the same professionalism and respect you treat them with. I like to say that "I go where I'm celebrated, not tolerated."

"Remember to always give people a reason to want to do business with you, and they will."

SUCCESS SNAPSHOT

PERSONAL SECURITY SERVICES

"Learn The People You're Dealing With"

INCOME: $20,000/month or more.

LICENSING: Check with your state. Most states regulate the security industry, and if you are a felon you likely will not be able to own or operate a security firm. You still may be able to work for one in an unarmed position.

TRAINING AND SPECIAL SKILLS: Self-defense training or combat training; have enough street and people skills to be good at conflict resolution; be able to mentally handle yourself in stressful situations, with split-second timing; keen observation skills.

EXPERIENCE: none needed.

START-UP COSTS: A bare minimum of about $10,000 which is mostly for insurance and initial payroll reserves while you wait for your customers to pay their billings.

There are many ways to make money providing security, and only a few of them involve carrying a gun. This is good news for ex-felons who cannot carry a firearm. If protecting people and property with common sense is your passion then owning a security company is worth considering. If you have control issues or are on a "power trip," stay away from security services (and go into law enforcement or corrections!?)

The purpose of security is to discretely prevent and contain bad situations while protecting people and property. Security is all about people. Whether you are containing a drunk at a bar, preventing a person from unauthorized access to an office building, or taking documents from one place to another, every act you do in security is protecting people or property from other people and sometimes from themselves.

There are four main ways to make money providing security. They are:

1. Protective services.
2. Body guard services.
3. Bonded guard and courier services (These almost always carry a gun, and sometimes have special vehicles and a large onsite safe).
4. Property protection.

You'd be surprised at the wide range of places and things that require security services. I don't think you can go through a whole day without encountering a place that uses security guards, either seen or unseen. Many businesses do a good job of having their security team blend in with other customers. Others, like banks and clubs, want their security to be obvious and high profile as a preventative measure.

I remember my first trip to Kenya. I went to a bank downtown to change dollars into their currency, Kenyan Shillings. At first I was shocked to see their security with machine guns. Later, I learned how frequent pick-pockets and robberies occurred. I was glad they were armed.

Here are a few places that use security services:

1. Weddings, parties, and special events.
2. Bars, restaurants, and clubs.
3. Concerts, plays, and sporting events.
4. Conventions.
5. High profile trips and visits by dignitaries, celebrities, the wealthy, and top level executives.
6. Retail stores, shopping malls, factories, and office buildings: both after-hours and during normal working hours.
7. Hotels, apartments, townhomes, and gated communities.
8. Money and document collection and delivery (usually armed).
9. Banks and financial institutions (usually armed).
10. Bodyguard and personal protective services.

Regardless of how you approach your business, to operate a security company the most important skills are:

1. Professionalism, reliability, and discretion. Your customer wants every situation to be diffused, without harm to person or property, and does not want an incident that would negatively impact their business or reputation.

2. Customer loyalty. Recognize your assignment is the most important thing in the world for your customer.

3. Basic self-defense, without a fear of taking control of a situation or dealing with a volatile situation. It's more about prevention than reaction. Prevention keeps problems from happening. Reaction is trying to put the cow back in the barn after it walked out to the pasture.

4. Conflict resolution and people skills. Remember, security is always, and ultimately only, about people and keeping them from doing things your client doesn't want to happen.

Security can be billed based on:
1. An hourly rate.
2. A daily, weekly, or monthly retainer.
3. By the event.

Be a "mystery shopper" and do market research into who your competition is and what they charge. Then, determine your costs to start, your operating expenses, and whether security could be a profitable adventure for you.

You would be surprised how inexpensive it can be to start a security operation. Your biggest expense will be your payroll. Make sure you have enough working capital (cash) on hand to pay payroll while you wait for your first billings to arrive.

Your next biggest expense will be insurance and rent for your office (if you have one). If you do "plain clothes security," have your workers dress according to the specific standards your clients want. Always be professional. You can also do "uniform" work at an added expense.

Here's a question for you about security: what is more important for a security guard to have, a gun or a radio (or phone)? In the old days, before everyone had a cell phone, security companies gave all of their officers a radio and usually had a central monitoring operation to for support. Now only the biggest security companies have a central monitoring station. A phone or a radio are far more important and powerful tools for the security guard to carry than a gun. No one can out run a phone or radio, but guns can miss and you never want a situation to escalate where you need to draw your weapon. You don't want a situation where you need a gun unless you are getting paid a *lot* of money!

PERSONAL SECURITY SERVICE: BARRY'S STORY, continued:

If you read the Success Snapshot on a Martial Arts Studio you know that Barry and his partners started and operated a successful martial arts studio that had a great reputation for self-defense training. Because of their reputation, a club owner asked them to provide security for his business. Soon they added other clubs and office buildings and quickly grew to twenty-five, part-time security officers and $20,000/month in extra income. All without adding additional support staff or space to their martial arts studio.

Barry says the key to his success was how he screened, hired, trained-- and the quality control they used to manage--their officers. His biggest piece of advice is to "learn the people you're dealing with." This holds true for employees and clients, but is especially true for patrons at the businesses and events you are paid to guard.

Barry hired people who loved to fight, but only fought as a last resort. They had to exhibit self-control, common sense, people skills, and have the street sense to be able to recognize an escalating situation and quickly take control of it before problems occurred. Problems can happen in a split-second. To properly protect people and property the security guard must have the mental ability to react quickly and handle stressful situations. When problems occur, the officers need discretion to protect the reputation of the business while protecting the people and property that are part of the security assignment.

It has been said that tests and obstacles only reveal the true person you are. Barry would send in his own "mystery shoppers" to test his workers while on duty. For instance, he would regularly send in friends that he paid to pretend they were drunk and try to create a scene to see how his guard would handle the situation. Barry is a hands-on kind of guy that felt there was no better way to train than to deal with real-life situations. By sending in his own mystery shoppers Barry could train and evaluate staff without exposure to a real life problem. There was no more valuable tool or marketing piece that Barry could have used.

Here is how "learning the people you are dealing with" helps you succeed in business:

With your staff: Isn't it amazing that everyone in a job interview is perfect? So how can you know how to hire the right person to work with you? More than just asking questions that people will give you an answer they think you want to hear, the best way to evaluate and train someone is to observe them and give them feedback. Before you hire someone, you should know what personality types, work traits, and skills you want to have onboard. Then, use your street smarts to find or develop that person into what you need. That is the best way to have a "match" and reduce employee turnover to weed out workers that aren't meeting your needs. Hire staff with the strengths you want them to have, and let them use their strengths.

With your client: you should know your client's motivations and what they want from you. It may seem obvious, but personalize your service by asking them questions like "What is most important to you for us to do? Is there anything extra we can be doing for you?" Going the extra mile distinguishes yourself from your competition and can be the reason someone accepts and keeps you.

With the customers at your client's business: Once you have the right workers in place and you have a clear idea what your client wants, then the most important part of being a security guard is guarding and observing everything to prevent issues. It sounds simple, but you would be surprised how many security services lose business and get a bad reputation because their guards spend more time socializing than observing and guarding. Having the mystery shopper helps, as does random visits by the boss on the job, and rotating your guards to different assignments periodically.

Learning the people you're dealing with makes you a better security professional, a better businessman, and a better person. It also makes you better prepared to succeed against your competition, who you should also know as well.

Leadership genius Dr. John C. Maxwell says: "The whole world, with one notable exception, is made up of others." So why not learn everything you can about the people that cross your path, in business and in life?

"The whole world, with one notable exception, is made up of others."

-John C. Maxwell

SUCCESS SNAPSHOT

DETAILING BUSINESS

"The Little Details Mean Everything"

INCOME: $20-$85/hour or more.

START-UP COSTS: $500 +/-.

SKILLS and TRAINING REQUIRED: a great attention to detail and speed cleaning skills will help you make more money detailing.

How often do you wash your car? According to data published by the United States Census Bureau, January 2014, the Car Wash Industry has $5.8 billion in annual sales. A vehicle is the second largest purchase most consumers will ever make. Regular washing protects that investment and makes driving more enjoyable. Many people barely have time for a car wash, much less regular detailing. According to a recent survey from gasbuddy.com:

> *"41% of people wash their car only when it's dirty, 18% wash it monthly, 18% wash it as a matter of pride of ownership."*

How often do you wax or detail your car? Some people love deep cleaning their car; others hate it. Who doesn't enjoy a clean car? A recent survey from the International Car Wash Association (ICA) claims that thirty-seven million cars smell because of interior garbage! Many would clean or care for their vehicle better if they had more time. Industry professionals recommend at least monthly car washes, unless needed earlier, and detailing at least two to four times a year to protect a vehicle from the elements. Clearly, there is a substantial market for cleaning and detailing cars, but cars aren't the only thing getting detailed.

Boats, motorcycles, RVs, campers, semi-tractor trailers, even airplanes all need professional detailing. That's why this section is called

"Detailing Business" as opposed to a "Car Detailing Business." Think outside the box and don't limit yourself to just cars or consumers either. Business owners are a huge source of revenue for you, especially if you provide credit terms and bill weekly or monthly.

Detailing is one of the easiest and cheapest businesses to start, but it is one that requires you to constantly hustle for business. You can make great money, especially if you grow enough to hire employees. To survive long enough to grow you must be reliable, professional, and give the customer a better, more-detailed cleaning than they could have done on their own. It's the little things, the attention to the smallest detail, that count the most.

One of my nephews made great money detailing vehicles, as did one of my best friends. Like graphic arts or lawn care it could be a good source of part-time income to help you launch another business.

You can have a mobile detailing business where you go to the customer and detail, or you pick up the vehicle and drive it back to your place. Car lots love using a mobile detail service as the better the cars look the better they sell. A study by Meguiar's indicates used cars with a glossy finish sell for at least $1,000 more than those with a dull finish. Many new and used car lots are outsourcing their detailing needs. Offer them a discounted price if they give you a regular number of cars each week to detail for them. Also offer them billing terms to get their business if you feel comfortable in their ability and willingness to pay you.

Here are twelve other ways, thinking outside the box, you can make money with a mobile detailing service:

1. Check with your local executive airport and local aircraft owner clubs. Small airplane owners, or the aircraft services that manage airplanes, need the planes' interior cleaned and the exterior waxed. Ask them if there are any special products they prefer you use on the airplanes.

2. Check with your local marinas and boat shops and offer your services. To promote your business you can even give boat shops a referral fee for sending you customers or discounts on gift certificates for your detailing service. The boat shop could give a gift certificate for a free detail to every customer who buys a boat. You might want to suggest this same promotion to car lots also.

3. Check with your local RV dealers and offer your services to them along with referral fees for them sending you customers. Repeat the gift certificate offer with them.

4. Offering discounts to motorcycle clubs and shops can get you established in that market. Repeat the referral fees and gift certificate offer with them.

5. Offer your services to car clubs and a discount to their members. Attend an event and pass out coupons or flyers. Be friendly.

6. Offer your services to trucking companies and independent truckers: especially over-the-road truckers.

7. Contact local car and truck rental companies and offer your services to them. Many have detailers on staff but you could be their cleaner when they are short-staffed or when they need to detail a vehicle quickly.

8. Contact local body shops and offer your services. Many have in-house detailers, but if they are happy with your work they could send you all their business, or use you for overflow detailing.

9. Place an ad on Craigslist and offer a price for detailing vehicles of private owners selling their own vehicles and those wanting a clean vehicle but who don't have the time for detailing.

10. Have customers and friends give you positive reviews on Yahoo, Google, Angie's List, and any online forum you come across.

11. Make a Facebook page for your business and send special offers to those that "like" your page or who are in your contact list.

12. Contact the human resource department of large corporations and let them know you are available to provide discount detailing to employees. You may arrange for a few parking spaces onsite, a water spigot, and a day you can schedule to wash and detail vehicles onsite. Some companies might even pay for all the detailing for their employees. Most won't do that, but many companies will love to provide a benefit to the workers that doesn't cost them anything. You may pick up new customers beyond the one-time detailing. If you hear of a company trying to raise money for a charity you can offer to donate a portion of your detailing you do onsite for their charity.

The second way to earn money detailing is to have a detailing shop where people come to you and drop off their vehicle, boat, RV, or motorcycle. This can be your own shop or perhaps you can share or sublet space with an auto body shop, parking garage, gas station, or a car dealership. You could offer them a certain amount of free details each month to work off your rent, or give them special pricing for each detail you perform for them. Having a shop will give you year-round income if you can afford it. Market your shop to the same group of customers as listed above.

Whether you offer a mobile detail service, or have a shop, your business likely will benefit from using Google AdWords. Do a market study to find out what detailing services are being offered in your market, what they charge, and what they specialize in. That will guide you in the direction your detailing business goes.

To price your services do the following:
1. Determine the wash and detail packages you will offer. For instance:

    Passenger cars, Interior
    Passenger cars, exterior with a wax, etc.
    SUVs and passenger trucks, Interior
    SUVs and passenger trucks, exterior with a wax

2. Establish a minimum price for each of the following and bid each project before you start it:

    Boats
    Airplanes
    Motorcycles - cruiser, road bike, racing bike, bike trailer, etc.
    Tractor Trailers, with a sleeper.
    Tractor Trailers, single cab.
    Special Projects

It's the little things that count the most, especially in the detailing business. Who would use a detailing business that didn't pay attention to the details, not just the details on the vehicle but also in your operation, like timeliness, professionalism, courtesy, and value? I love detailing my vehicles when I have time. When I don't have time, I'll use a professional detailing service. I expect that service to do as good as or better work than I would if I detailed it myself. Here are some of the little details I look for when I get a vehicle professionally detailed:

- Clean the inside and outside of windows with no overspray.
- Perfectly clean headlights, taillights, mirrors, and sidelights.
- Have an even amount of dressing on the dashboard, plastics, and leather with no pooling of extra product.
- Make sure the air vents are perfectly clean. This requires hand work with a Q-tip or small brush.
- Perfectly clean wheels and wheel wells.
- Make sure there is consistent coverage of tire dressing.
- Avoid extra swirls anywhere on the paint surface.
- Have all chrome polished with no cloudy portions or dried wax on it.
- I look for cleaned and waxed door jambs with dressing on the interior door trim.
- Most importantly make sure there is no extra wax or product on the edges of metal on the inside of door jambs, edges of the hood and trunk, trim around headlight and taillights, or joints between body parts like where the quarter panel meets the door.

Also consider your image. Dress for success; even (and especially) while detailing vehicles. Someone who cares enough for their vehicle to have it detailed wants to be able to trust the person they hire to detail it. Have a professional appearance that gives your customers confidence. When you can afford it, wear a uniform with your logo on it. Pick consistent shorts or pants to wear, like khaki cargo shorts or work pants. Make paying attention to those details the thing that separates you from the crowd. If you are a mobile service, don't show up in a dirty vehicle. If you have a shop, make sure the waiting area, work area, and any area the customer can see is very clean, well-lit, and comfortable. It all build customer confidence in your work.

The list below includes much of what you need to start, most of which is readily available at your local auto parts store or online. Only use products designed for professional detailing. Buy the best products you can afford. Whatever products you use, Google them for product reviews.

Meguiar's DA Power System includes their Ultimate Rubbing Compound, Ultimate Polish, Ultimate Wax, three grades of polishing foam pads for use in a drill or buffer, and microfiber towels. Also get:

- Polo shirts or tee shirts with your company logo on them for you to give a great first impression.

- A good electric powered vacuum as battery powered ones don't clean well enough for professional detailing.
- A decent drill and/or buffer.
- Buffing pads of varying thickness and type for stripping, using rubbing compound, using clay bars, and waxing.
- Extension cords to power your vacuum, drill and/or buffer, and power washer.
- Cleaning buckets.
- A tray or basket to professionally organize, store, and carry your products: whether a mobile service or a shop.
- Professional chamois.
- Microfiber towels and professional grade paper towels.
- Trash bags and plastic bags to cover the alternator if you are washing the engine.
- Car wash concentrate, like Meguiar's Wash and Wax.
- Rubbing compound.
- A great wax.
- Professional grade glass cleaner.
- Wheel cleaner, like Hot Rims Tire and Wheel Cleaner.
- Tire dressing, like Endurance Tire Spray.
- A product to clean and dress plastic, rubber, and vinyl as in dashboards, steering wheels, seals, seats, and floor mats.
- Chrome polish.
- A good degreaser concentrate, for use on the wheel wells, under carriage, and engine cleaning.
- Spray bottles.
- Leather cleaner and conditioner.
- Carpet cleaner/spot cleaner.
- Cleaning brushes, scrub brushes, little detail brushes
- Q-Tips.
- Rubber gloves.
- Sponges.
- Paper liners for the flooring after you finish an interior detail.
- Clay bars (if you intend on offering restorative detailing).

For a nice extra touch you can ask your customer what their preference is in air freshener. Staple a business card or coupon to the air freshener so they can remember you for referrals and future business.

Later, if your business needs it, you may want to invest in:
- A power washer.
- A carpet cleaner.
- A Hotsy or a steam cleaner (for cleaning engines and things).

It's the little details that will set you apart from your competition, and will make your customers remember you.

> *"The little details mean everything."*

SUCCESS SNAPSHOT

MAKE MONEY SUBLEASING PROPERTY, WITHOUT (OR WITH) OWNING REAL STATE

"Leaders Aren't Paid To Take Risks: We Are Paid To Take Risks Worth Taking."

"Thinking Outside The Box Can Create Opportunities For You That Others Miss."

This is another Success Snapshot based on my own business and investment experience. You don't have to own real estate to make a lot of money renting it. You can make a nice business from renting a larger space and breaking it into smaller pieces or a shared rental. This works whether you own the real estate or not. If you don't own the space then your lease needs to give you the right to sublease portions of it without your landlord's approval. Most landlords won't care as long as you remain actively responsible for the whole space you are renting.

Even if you are not trying to make a business out of subletting, subletting space is a great way to help your primary business make more money, lower your overhead, or lease bigger space. For instance, let's say you started an auto body shop and there is a building you want to be in that is a little larger than what you need but otherwise is perfect for you. You could afford to rent it all yourself but you don't want to have all of your money go towards rent. Instead, you find a detail shop to share space. You can barter/trade rent for car details or charge them rent. Renting to them not only helps lower your overhead and make more money it gives you greater flexibility for expansion. Now you have the space to expand into when your business grows, but until then, you don't have dead weight pulling your profits down.

Here's how I stumbled into making big money from subletting space. As a commercial real estate broker I once took a sales listing of a small well-located commercial strip center in the inner city. My client was an out-of-town owner who had held the property for a long time and had long-term tenants. It was a brick building with great parking, a new roof, but a lack of updates and maintenance kept the rents low. It was on one of the busiest streets in town with good visibility, full access from all directions, and in the middle of a densely populated neighborhood. I believed in the property and thought it had great upside potential.

Whether working with a buyer, investor, or a tenant I always looked for the best deals. Usually the best deals are properties that have been on the market a while, or are otherwise distressed like in a foreclosure or divorce.

Isn't it ironic that everyone wants a property, a business, or an investment with upside potential but hardly anyone wants something that is less than perfect or needs some work, fixing, adjusting, or updating? If the property, the business, or the deal were perfect, the price would be higher, the seller wouldn't be selling it, or someone else would've already bought it. Despite how many infomercials you watch the only way to make money in real estate, any business, or any investment is to buy it for the best price possible then work hard, fix the problems, and run a tight ship. You hope the price reflects its condition and risk. That is how you "make money on the buy," which is rule #17 in Pelshaw's Principles of Profitable Business (Appendix E).

Leaders aren't paid to take risks, we are paid to take risks worth taking. There is more risk taking on someone else's problems. You lessen and manage that risk by doing your homework on the business or investment so you know exactly what you're getting into. Then you make sure the effort and investment of your time, talent, and treasure into the adventure is worth what you are expecting in profit.

> *"Leaders aren't paid to take risks:*
> *We are paid to take risks worth taking."*
>
> *-Pelshaw's Principles of Profitable Business*

I've always made my money solving problems and I saw this property as an opportunity.

I bought it for 95 percent of the list price and quickly spent money catching up on needed repairs. We cleaned up the landscape, applied a new coat of asphalt for the parking lot, and we painted the building's trim. Whenever I paint a building, I like to change the color for people to realize something new and improved is going on there. After the building had new "lipstick" (cosmetic improvements) I started raising the rents.

One of the three rental bays in the building was a large barber shop paying $1,250/month rent, the other a small hair salon paying $300/month rent. The hair salon was a poorly-run operation that desperately needed updating. I chose to not renew their lease so I could update the bay and re-rent it to a better tenant for more money. I replaced the ceiling tiles, lights, laid a new ceramic floor, repainted everything and updated the bathrooms. It looked great. I happened across an ad for a hair salon that was selling its equipment. I bought a large wall unit that accommodated four cosmetologist work stations. I also bought two professional hair dryer chairs, four salon chairs, waiting area chairs, and a display cabinet. I wanted to rent the bay as a furnished salon for $600/month which was a bargain given the location, condition, and being fully equipped.

I was totally amazed that every barber or cosmetologist that looked at the bay loved it, but all of them asked me if I would rent them a chair for $100 per week. I told them I wasn't in the salon business but since there were four chairs why don't they rent the shop for $600, charge $100/week for the three other chairs/rental booths, and make $1,200 from renting the other three chairs/rental booths? Nobody saw it that way and they all were afraid to lease the whole shop.

At the time everyone asked me to lease them a chair I was still stuck in my traditional landlord mode. All I wanted was rent money from the space: I wasn't yet thinking outside the box on ways to maximize income from my property. Soon I was forced to think outside the box. It was very profitable and it solved problems. If I hadn't been adaptable I would've missed a great opportunity.

About the same time I was trying to lease the remodeled bay, my barber shop tenant was a month late in paying the rent. I tried calling the shop owner but never reached anyone and finally the phone was disconnected. I decided to visit the shop and ran into Robert the manager. The shop was busy and appeared profitable. I asked Robert where his boss was and Robert told me "he went to jail for a long time but am I glad to see you. I have your chair rental money for you." He tried to give me $2,500 in cash so I decided to let him know the shop only owed one month's rent. He said he understood that but that everyone in the shop was on the chair rental arrangement and that was the money he was holding for me.

I told him "Robert that's way more than the rent for this place, why don't you take over the shop yourself." His response shocked me: "I don't think I can handle covering the rent, phone, and utilities and things but I'll manage it for you if you want, and I can even fill up the empty bay you've been trying to rent."

It was at that moment we took a bay that rented for $1,250/month and cleared $2,500/month from it. We took a bay I couldn't rent for $600/month and got $1,600/month rent from that. After that I took three other commercial spaces I had been trying to lease and repeated the same formula with the same results. Two of the bays turned into other beauty salons and the other space was leased to various family counselors as a shared professional office.

Whether you are a barber, cosmetologist, nail tech, massage therapist, lawyer, accountant, business owner, family counselor, woodworking shop owner, art gallery, or a gym, there is a lot of money to be made by sharing space with others and subleasing. Look for well-located large space that you can share or divide with other business professionals. Not every landlord will allow you to sublease their space, but landlords of properties that have been vacant for a long time will be the most open to this idea.

Lease the space first, then use your income to buy it. Unless you want to buy it anyway, I advise people to lease the space so you can build up your cash flow and "try it before you buy it." Then use your profits from subleasing or business operations to purchase the property.

Renting a smaller space from a bigger space should always be at a rate higher per square foot than what the whole lease costs. Factor in the pro-rata expenses like utilities, cable, and cleaning, and the risk you take for being responsible for the rent due on the entire space. Ideally, you should have interested parties before you take the plunge on rental property to sublease.

You can sign a lease for a property subject to your ability to sublease it. Make sure you receive, in writing, permission to market and show the space for three to six months or however long you can get. To make the landlord agree with you, let them know you will share all potential subleasing leads with them if you walk away from the deal. What do they have to lose, especially if their property was vacant for a while?

Taking a larger bay and subleasing part of it is a great way to help you get space for your business to grow. You have the income from the extra space while you start out and you have the option to grow into it as your business grows. That makes a win-win situation for you.

Whether you are a landlord or a tenant you can make money leasing a larger space and subletting it into smaller pieces as long as you don't mind the management and risk of the overhead for the whole space while you sublet the remaining space. You can even negotiate a lease that gives you an option to purchase the property. Use your subleasing income to buy the property. This type of land-lording requires extra screening, extra diligence, and constant communication with your tenant. If you don't stay on top of it disasters will occur and you will be left holding the bag for their unpaid rent and any damages.

I know of a friend who rents nice office space, hires a receptionist, provides a conference room, copy machine, fax machine, wireless internet, and rents individual office suites. This is usually called "executive office space" and is an industry in and of itself. She takes space she leases for $10/SF and subleases it for $25/SF. What she charges for the shared receptionist, and photocopies usually comes close to covering her expenses (other than rent) and she has a profitable business.

My friend Chad does with houses what I was doing with commercial space: he buys a rental home, and instead of renting it to one tenant, he'll rent the bedrooms to individuals and set them up as roommates. He will rent a four-bedroom house that may get $1000/month rent to four separate roommates at $550/month utilities paid with cable and internet. He has to pay the utilities, but still clears $800 more than he would get renting it individually. This type of land-lording is not for everyone. You have to screen tenants and stay in constant contact with them or disaster will occur. If you are willing to put the extra effort in managing the rental you can make great money.

Thinking outside the box can create opportunities for you that others miss. Whatever business you start, you should consider looking for space to sublet or share. This is a great strategy to save you money, help build your business, and give you options to aid in your expansion.

SUCCESS SNAPSHOT

MOBILE HOMES

"Think Outside The Box By Renting Them"

We've all heard jokes about mobile homes.

"Did you hear they cancelled the Parade of Homes in Okmulgee? The trailer got a flat tire."

"How are a divorce and a tornado the same in Okmulgee? In both events you lose the trailer."

There is no offense intended to anyone from Okmulgee or anybody who has lived in a trailer. If anything these jokes show the unfair treatment mobile homes have gotten in the past. Modern mobile and modular homes are far better constructed than their predecessors, and many have amenities that rival more expensive stick-built homes.

As residential lending for housing continues to tighten, conventional home ownership will continue to decline. Since The Great Recession (2009 onward) homeownership has declined from 67 percent to about 60 percent of the households in the United States according to the US Census Bureau. Mobile homes will continue to be a growing part of providing housing for families in the future.

There are several things about the mobile home business that fascinate me:

1. How they are an effective and affordable housing option for many people, especially in booming areas and rural areas.

2. How cheaply they can be bought, whether new or used.

3. How quickly new ones lose value (depreciate).

4. The money that can be made on them.

I had a client that was a mobile and modular home dealer, and he taught me a lot about that industry. Since that time I've often toyed with several business concepts using mobile homes that I will share with you here.

There are three ways to make money from mobile homes:

1. Owning a mobile home park, renting the individual slips out and/or renting out actual mobile homes as well.

2. Buying and selling mobile homes, both new and used.

3. Owning mobile homes that you rent, even sometimes sell.

Owning a Mobile Home Park

As a developer I've considered developing or buying a mobile home park. They usually are great money makers if you can acquire them for the right price. Owning a park gives you the best chance to buy mobile homes at distressed prices from motivated sellers, because the mobile homes are already parked on your lot. Why spend money to disconnect it and move it when you can sell it quickly and cheaply to the park? The park can then clean it up, resell it or rent it, all hopefully at a profit.

Because of how shabby some mobile home parks have become, many cities have forced poorly run mobile home parks to close. Some mobile homes parks were in the path of development, so they sold out to be converted to other uses. The end result is there are fewer places to put mobile homes, with strong, maybe even increasing, demand for park rental space. Most cities require new mobile home parks to have what's called "Restrictive Covenants." These covenants are designed to govern the condition of homes in the parks and sometimes the age of the homes allowed. Some covenants limit the number of rental units that can be in a park what a resident can do to the outside of their trailer. The best parks have guidelines that state that trailers should be permanently mounted with skirting.

Buying and Selling Mobile Homes

You don't have to own a park to buy and sell mobile homes. New mobile home dealers often take used trailers in on trade. You'd be surprised how cheaply you can buy some of these used trailers. The other thing you'll be surprised with is how quickly a new mobile home loses value once it's moved from the sales lot. A new mobile home can depreciate as fast as a new car does once it's taken off the sales lot.

Auctions and mobile home dealers are great sources to buy mobile homes from. Also check Craigslist and your local mobile home parks for deals on mobile homes you can buy. Once you get a good mobile home that you can buy for the right price, then you can decide to sell it or lease it with an option to purchase.

Renting Mobile Homes

Think outside the box and make money renting one! It could be a lot easier to get into the rental business using mobile homes, if you have a lot or land you can lease that allows you to rent the mobile home. Because they depreciate in value so quickly you can purchase a good mobile home in need of cosmetic upgrades. I have friends that achieve a one to three year payback on their investment when they buy, fix up, and rent out mobile homes. They are very careful to not overpay when they buy a used mobile home, and they carefully screen and manage their tenants.

Are you ready to make money outside of the box by trying something different?

SUCCESS SNAPSHOT

RENTAL BUSINESS

"What's Your Toll Bridge?"

"Treat Your Customers Like Friends And Soon They Will Be"

"Be A Part Of The Community"

"Get Expert Advice - It Pays For Itself In The Long And Short Run"

"You Don't Need To Go To Business School Or College, But You Do Need To Have A Good Plan And Stick To It To Succeed"

Warren Buffet once said that he thought the best investment was a toll bridge. They have a one-time investment with continual cash flow. That sounds exactly like the rental business to me. I have always loved the concept of a rental business. I'm not referring to real estate here, but I am referring to almost everything else such as:

Tools	Construction equipment	Party supplies
Scaffolding	Cars or trucks	Trailers
Tuxedos	Wedding dresses	Costumes
Audio equipment	Instruments	Games
Trampolines	Computers	Snow mobiles
Boats	Canoes	Motorcycles
Snowboards/skis	Bicycles	Bouncy houses
Exercise equipment	Furniture	Tractor Trailer

All rental businesses share the same basic premise, similar to Buffet's toll bridge. You continue to make money on an item you've bought only once.

People and businesses rent items for one or more of the following reasons:

1. They fulfill a specific need or purpose.
2. Some things are rented because are used only once or twice, like a tuxedo, wedding dress, or moving trailer.
3. It is cheaper to rent it than to buy it.
4. The rental shop location is more convenient for them than using their own equipment, such as ski and snowboard rentals at a ski resort, or canoe rental at a river or lake.

WAYNE'S STORY:

Wayne had a great job as an assistant buyer for a high-end Los Angeles retailer. He on the way up the corporate ladder, drove a Porsche, and lived the good life. Unfortunately part of the "good life" included partying hard. Soon the partying became out of control and Wayne had a stern wakeup call. He attended the funeral of his best friend who overdosed. Wanting to get away from the party scene and the pressures of his corporate life, Wayne needed a fresh start. He always loved the mountains but wanted to get far enough away from Southern California that he wouldn't be tempted to regress into his old life. So off to Colorado it was.

Wayne worked for a ski rental shop as a boot fitter and loved it, despite its low pay. When the season was over, so was the job. At that time the best paying jobs in the valley were driving trucks for the mines. So Wayne got his CDL and was hired to drive a truck for the local mine. He drove for a few years, saving money and making friends with the locals along the way.

Wayne had a friend who made money buying and selling used ski equipment and clothing. This friend also was a top-notch ski tuner with a great reputation as a racing coach. His friend had tremendous connections among the locals. Wayne and his friend learned of a small well-located ski tuning shop that wanted out of the business. They approached that shop and was able to buy them out of their lease and assume their remaining lease obligation. They did not buy their business, just their lease.

Wayne's partner used his connections to approach other ski rental shops. They bought end-of-season and used equipment for pennies on the dollar. This was their initial inventory. They budgeted to replace equipment every three years. They continued to buy used equipment and some new equipment during their operation.

There were several ski rental shops in their town, but Wayne's partner's ski tuning and coaching expertise distinguished them as the premier shop for serious skiers. They were the only shop that advertised race tuning and hand tuning. Wayne used his friendships and relationships he maintained in Los Angeles, many of whom worked in the entertainment industry, to build business for their shop, too. So they had the business from the locals and from the entertainment and party crowd from L.A. Did I mention Wayne's shop was in Aspen, Colorado?

Wayne and his partner tried to distinguish themselves in other ways such as the level of training they gave their workers, their highly personal customer service, and what they did to respect and appreciate the locals. Every year on the last day of the season Wayne held "The First Annual Fire Sale" at which he had a radio station, band, and all the free food and alcohol you could handle, along with great deals on new and gently used equipment. Being innovative, Wayne's shop was the first to offer mountain bike rentals and to expand to other types of rentals and sales.

I asked Wayne what advice he had for a new business owner. Here's what Wayne says:

1. Develop a business plan, and stick to it. After being open for a few years they realized they were great with the equipment and tuning, but they weren't the best business managers. Wayne hired a business management firm to come in to create a solid business plan and monthly support to implement it. Business quickly increased. The management company not only paid for itself, but also gave them a return on their investment. He wishes he engaged them earlier, despite the fact that getting the data and records they needed to do their job was difficult for Wayne and his partner to do since they weren't the most organized businessmen. He said he learned more from his management consultant than he did from college.

2. To survive, offer something your competition doesn't and promote it.

3. Be a member of your community, not just someone pulling money from the community. The "First Annual Fire sale" was part of their way of giving back to their community.

4. Keep a cushion of operating capital (cash) of at least six months expenses. You never know when it rain, but you do know it always will!

And the most important advice from Wayne on doing business:

> *"Treat your customers like friends,*
> *and soon they will be."*
>
> *-Wayne*

SUCCESS SNAPSHOT

SUBCONTRACTOR, CONTRACTOR, OR BUILDER

"Work 'ON' The Business As Much As 'IN' The Business."

"Sometimes You Have To Stand Up For Your Integrity."

"Organize Or Agonize: Preparation Is The Key To Your Success."

This applies to any type of construction subcontracting or contracting such as, but not limited to:

Carpenter	Framing Carpenter
Finish/Trim Carpentry	Cornice Carpenter
Stair Carpenter	Soffit Carpenter
Deck Builder	Outdoor Living Carpenter
Painter	Handyman
Drywall hanger	Drywall finisher
Cement Layer	Mason
Block layer	EIFS Subcontractor
Siding installer	Roofer
Caulking Subcontractor	Wallpaper Installer
Insulation Contractor	Window & Door Installer
Grading Contractor	Security Alarm Installer
Sound System Specialist	Fences
Water proofer	Sprinklers
Landscaping	Garage Door Contractor

INCOME: $35/hour up to $1,000/day or more.

TRAINING/EDUCATION: You need to know the trade you want to work in even if all you are doing is subbing out to other crews. You should possess enough knowledge to be an expert in your field to your customer. The list of subs and contractors above are not licensed trades like electricians, plumbers, or HVAC contractors, but this example applies to them as well. Even if you haven't been to school for it, you should be able to learn the trade you want to do by working for a good employer that is willing to train you. You can also go to a good trade school but they won't ever teach you as much as you could learn from an employer who wants you to succeed.

WHAT YOU NEED TO START:

Whatever tools and equipment you need for your particular trade. You can equip yourself to practice most trades for $2,000 - $5,000 in tools if you buy good used tools from garage sales, Craigslist, other contractors, and pawn shops. When you learn your trade you will know exactly what tools and equipment you need to start. You can borrow or rent tools and equipment until you can afford to buy your own.

Being a subcontractor is a great way for many to get into business for themselves. It's one of the easiest businesses to start if you know what you're doing. Whether it's painting, carpentry, drywall, or installing sprinklers, all subcontracting requires mastery of a skill. It helps if the business you are trying to start is a task other trades or people don't like performing.

I have a friend whose company only does the final detail work on bricks, block, and precast concrete that other masonry contractors don't do because they like laying the masonry, not cleaning it up. His customers leave the last 2-5 percent of a job for my friend's company to come behind and finish. My friend grosses about a million dollars a year doing the part of the job masons don't like!

Have you ever thought about how many different people and different subcontractors work on a house being built? The previous list has more than thirty different contractors or subcontractors, not counting the builder. There were more I could've have listed also.

Did you notice carpentry had seven categories? Why isn't one category sufficient? Specialization. Gone are the days of one company that does everything. A general contractor may sub out the framing; the framing contractor may sub out the steps and cornice work; the painting contractor may sub out the caulking or the taping; and on and on it goes. Specialization gives the opportunity to focus on your strengths and passions, and create your own "purple cow" (unique selling proposition).

That's what my friend Ron did. Ron started with nothing, and became a very successful contractor and builder in Texas employing about 100 workers at his peak. He'll be the first to tell you just because you have workers and jobs, that does not mean you're making money. It's all about being organized, synchronized, and mobilized.

RON'S STORY:

Ron came from a large family that valued hard work and accomplishment. When Ron graduated high school he worked for an old Czech framer who taught Ron the basics of framing houses. Ron immediately took to carpentry "like a fish took to water." During college Ron had other jobs, but nothing gave him the joy and fulfillment that carpentry did.

I asked Ron why he excelled at carpentry and he said it was simply because he was doing what he loved. Ron said because of his passion for his work and his desire to learn more, his bosses noticed. They then taught him the trade and the business. That was a perfect example of the teacher appearing once the student was ready. Ron never felt like he knew everything, no matter how skilled he became. He tried to learn something from everyone he came in contact with, whether above or below him. To learn, Ron had to be prepared with the questions to ask.

Ron watched how his bosses ran their business and how they dealt with their clients. He tried hard to figure out their "system" for running a framing business. Soon Ron was supervising a crew for his boss and continuing to learn the business. He loved and appreciated his boss, and felt the right boss was a major key to his success in the business. Ron believed he had a higher purpose than just running a crew, so why not start his own company?

When Ron started his framing company he had a new family and was in his mid-20s. He drove a beat-up old Honda and was able to scrape together $2,000 to buy the tools he needed. He didn't have any work scheduled or lined up, nor did he have a truck. His first crew was a brother, his friend, and two college friends. To get work he approached smaller builders and other framers hoping to help them catch up from being behind. He didn't have any luck with the "big boys." Ron quickly made a reputation of on-time, quality work.

Ron made his company unique in his field by dedicating himself to making sure his clients (builders and other framers) made more money because they worked with Ron. That was Ron's "purple cow." Here are three things Ron gave his customers that most other framers didn't:

1. Ron had the cleanest job sites. He made each of his workers spend 10-15 minutes at the end of the day cleaning and organizing the job site. This made the builders they worked for feel better about the job. More importantly, it kept the job organized and quality control high.

2. <u>Ron made efficient use of materials.</u> When a builder or general contractor bids a project they estimate the material needed to complete it. If they went over and needed more material, the builders made less money. Other framers often made their clients buy more wood, usually because they were too lazy to use up scrap wood onsite. Ron's workers used as much scrap wood as possible. He bragged that he would have the smallest waste piles on a job site and the smallest instance of needing his customers to order more lumber. His customers noticed, and Ron was able to charge more for jobs because of the savings and extra profit he made for his customers.

3. <u>Ron would get his jobs done on time or early.</u> No matter how much his clients pressured him he never let them push him into making a commitment he couldn't keep. Ron always built in a few extra work days as a protection when he could.

Here are some important tips from Ron on how to be successful as a sub-contractor:

1. <u>Learn the skills.</u> Apprentice for a boss that wants you to learn and grow, and learn all aspects of the trade *and* the business. Running the business is a skill, too. Being skilled in the field won't make any difference if you don't promote your business, manage your business, or try to grow your business. Make sure you always do quality work. Your reputation is on the line.

2. <u>It's not when you start, it's when you finish that counts.</u> The companies Ron worked for would push Ron to start framing their house as soon as possible. Sounds good, right? Most subcontractors would start a job, to make their client happy, but often would pull off to finish something else. The client, who first was happy to see the job start, would get mad that the job wasn't progressing. Because of his integrity, Ron refused to do business that way. He wouldn't start a job until he was ready to give it his full attention. He would argue with clients at first, saying "it doesn't matter when I start, but when do you need it finished?" He lived this way, and trained his crews this way. Sometimes he even had to tell customers that if they didn't like the fact that he wasn't starting the job yet that they should find another framer. No customers replaced Ron, and he made sure the job was finished before the date the customer needed it. Because he was giving it his full attention, Ron often finished jobs *weeks* before other framers did, meaning Ron's crews could do more work and

make a lot more money. Ron wasn't wasting time or money juggling jobs, and his stress level was much less than when he was juggling jobs.

It took a while for Ron to train his clients that he wasn't going to let them down. Over time Ron earned his clients' trust, but they paid him more because they knew Ron would be on time, have a better organized job site, and have a lower lumber budget. Ron's customers would make more money because they used Ron's company.

3. <u>Organize or agonize: Preparation is the key to success.</u> Get the plans for the project as early as you can. If the first time you look at the plans is your first day on the job then two things will happen: 1) you will have guys standing around, and 2) you will make costly mistakes that will have to be redone, at your expense.

Ron realized that building was a process of blending a smaller system or task into a bigger system or task. Therefore, you must be organized to know your place and what you relate to on the project. To accomplish this, Ron would pour over every set of plans and study every detail before he submitted his bid and work schedule. Ron said you must spend several hours knowing the plans and visualizing the finished product before you ever bid or start the job. It takes the surprises out of the job.

Before he started a job he reviewed the plans with his lead worker/foreman for that job and they agreed on which worker would perform each task. Ron would make only one person responsible for reading and interpreting the plans and he wouldn't allow the whole crew to interpret plans. Other framing companies didn't have that control and often costly mistakes and delays were made by his competition because there wasn't clear leadership in the field.

Ron hired and trained the best workers he could find and assigned them their tasks on the crew based on their strengths. When Ron's crews arrived on site it was like watching a ballet, since everyone knew where to go and what to do because they were organized and trained to not stand around. Because they were prepared, they had very few field mistakes to correct. Correcting errors can sink a small company, so do the work right the first time.

Another reason for success: Ron organized his jobs by task, not by time. For instance, he would tell his workers "today we're going to frame all the exterior walls then we're done for the day." Even if it only took a half-day to complete they were still paid for the whole day. Being task-oriented instead of time-oriented also helped his crews to not stand around like some hourly workers do.

4. <u>Work well with others</u>. Ron trained his crews to work well with other subcontractors. Being easy to work with got him more business. If you do good work and people like working with you, customers will find you because of your reputation.

5. <u>Work "on" your business as much as you do "in" your business</u>. Even though he was framing, Ron's job was to make sure the business was being taken care of. Every day he filed receipts, made sales calls, submitted bids, reviewed his bills, studied plans, returned calls and emails, and handled his business.

6. <u>Make your customer's life easier, and they make your life easier</u>. Ron went out of his way to provide top quality work, to work well with other subcontractors on a job site, and to anticipate and fix problems for his customers, even if it wasn't his responsibility.

If you have talent and a will you can succeed, even if you start with nothing.

> *"Work ON the business as much as IN the business."*
>
> *-Ron. S.*

SUCCESS SNAPSHOT

PAWN SHOP

"Turn Your Inventory"

START-UP COSTS: At least $100,000 - $350,000 or more depending on if you focus on retail sales or loans, how large your operation will be, whether you do check cashing, and whether you buy a pawn shop franchise or start one from scratch.

LICENSING REQUIRED: All states require pawn shops to be licensed and follow specific laws. Many of these laws protect you and the public from people pawning stolen goods. In some states you can receive a pawn license if you are a felon if you do not handle guns or weapons in your pawn operation. Check with the agency in your state that issues pawn shop licenses. Licenses are issued by the State Department of Banking and Finance, the Secretary of State, or another department. Your state's official website will have the information you need.

Have you watched any of the reality TV shows about pawn shops? My favorite reality show is *Pawn Stars*. I liked it so much I appeared on the "Lord of the Ring" episode from the 2012 season.

Have you ever pawned something? Chances are you have, or you know someone who has. Who wouldn't want to own a pawn shop? You buy inventory cheap, your customers give you a high interest rate on what they borrow, and if they don't pay you back you keep and sell the pawned item that secures their loan.

Do you play poker? Do you have a "poker face?" Is it easy for you to say "no," or are you a pushover? Do you like to "wheel and deal?" Do you know a lot about jewelry, electronics, tools, and musical instruments? You might make a good pawn broker.

Not all pawns shops are the same, obviously. Did you know there are many different ways to make money owning a pawn shop? I learned this while servicing a client that owned a franchise territory for one of the world's leading pawn shops chains. I handled all of his real estate for him for a while, and much of what I pass on to you here is what I learned while working with him.

The two basic types of pawn shops are:

1. Pawn Shops that focus mostly on making money from loans, secured by pawned items. These count on pawn customers redeeming their pawned items. They still make money on retail sales, but usually their retail items aren't priced to sell like the other kind of pawn shop. My client's pawn shop focused on making money from loans. He told me to meet his "break-even point" he needed to maintain a book of loans of at least $100,000/month. He grossed $17,000/month on his book. "Break-even point" is the amount of money you need to earn to cover all of your overhead and expenses.

2. Pawn Shops that use their loans to buy low-cost inventory and then make a lot of money selling the pawned retail products that didn't get picked up. These shops have their sales inventory priced more aggressively because they want to turn their inventory quickly.

"Inventory turn" or just plain "turn" means the number of times in a year that a store will sell out its inventory. General merchandise retailers like Walmart or Target want to turn their inventory about six or more times per year. A car lot may turn its inventory three times per year. Stores that sell lower priced items, seasonal items, items that spoil, or have a shelf life all want to turn the inventory over quickly. Stores with bigger ticket items or items with a longer shelf life usually aren't as concerned about turning the inventory aggressively.

Every store should be concerned about inventory turn for several important reasons. Inventory represents a big investment of your money that isn't working for you while sitting on the shelves.

There is an art to retailing which is knowing how high (or how low) you can price an item to sell quickly without harming your profit. You can actually hurt your company by pricing something too low or too high. You can intentionally price something very low to get people in the door and make up profit based on whatever else you sell them. Grocery stores do this a lot. This is called a "loss leader" strategy. Here's an example: Advertise "$1 gallon of milk with $50 purchase." The $1 gallon of milk gets people in the door; the $50 minimum purchase helps make money. If you use a loss leader, make sure you have the item you advertise or someone may make a "bait and switch" complaint with your county attorney or attorney general.

In my opinion the best pawn shops turn their inventory as quickly as possible and still make money on outstanding loans.

Most pawn shops focus on the lower- to middle-income market, but there are pawn shops that target high-income households as well. Those that focus on high-income households pawn much larger ticket items, like very expensive jewelry, art, collectibles, cars, boats, or planes. These high-end pawn shops are not taking used DVDs or gaming cartridges.

Many pawn shops have added a check cashing operation inside the store. This can make you a lot of money also, but it requires a lot more capital. You must also be careful of the skilled check forgers and those that create checks on their computers that are so realistic they're difficult to tell they are fraudulent.

If you are going to own a pawn shop you and your staff need to be knowledgeable about a wide range of products. Anything you buy you should know enough about to buy and sell at a profit. The pawn industry has a large amount of reference material and websites you can subscribe to that give you information about nearly everything you can pawn. But certain things you can't look up, like whether the ring you are looking at has real diamonds or is a good cubic zirconium. Is that necklace silver plated, silver alloy, or sterling silver? There are training and tests available to teach you the basics of nearly anything you would pawn in your shop.

If you turn your inventory and your book of loans, you can't but help to make a lot of money in this industry. Isn't the purposing of retailing to sell things instead of collecting inventory?

SUCCESS SNAPSHOT

ENERGY AUDITOR

"Make Green By Going Green"

INCOME RANGE: $75,000 - $200,000/year or more.

TRAINING REQUIRED: A two-week class, field work, often with a test for certification.

RECOMMENDED READING: *Residential Energy* and the *Energy Auditor Field Guide"* by John Krigger are the "Bibles" of this industry.

EDUCATION REQUIRED: None other than the required Training.

ESTIMATED START-UP COSTS: $7,000 +/-.

PHYSICAL REQUIREMENTS: The ability to move and climb a step ladder and testing equipment, and lift up to seventy-five pounds.

SKILLS REQUIRED: The ability to handle paperwork for audit reimbursements and audit reports; ability to do the field inspections.

NECESSARY TO INCORPORATE: No.

How would you like to earn $1,500 - $5,000 or more per week, legitimately? Perhaps the growing field of energy auditing is for you. I must thank my friend whom we'll call "Ed" who helped me with the data and inspiration for this section.

In the last few years the government, along with local utilities and some non-profit groups, have been providing homeowners with financial incentives to help their homes be more energy efficient. The energy auditing industry was born to accommodate this growing trend. With rising utility costs and momentum from the green movement, the demand for energy auditing should continue to grow. In many cities the homeowner is reimbursed the cost of the energy audit. How hard would it be to sell a product that doesn't cost the customer anything, but could possibly save them thousands of dollars? Every homeowner is a possible customer. Now you see the huge potential and the great money that can be easily earned in this growing field.

Check the website dsire.org, your local utility, or your state's energy office to find out what financial incentives are offered in your area. Many states and utilities offer homeowners rebates and grants of $500 - $2,000 or more, as well as low-interest loans for homeowners making energy efficient improvements.

Energy auditors are paid to inspect and test homes and identify ways to improve energy efficiency. Each audit involves an on-site inspection and a follow-up visit to deliver and explain the results of the energy audit. The whole process can take 3- 4 hours for which you should be paid between $300 and $600 depending on the size and scope of the audit assignment and any reimbursement provided for the audit costs.

My friend Ed, by himself, does five to ten reports a week. According to Ed, the industry average is three reports per week, but not every energy auditor gives the business their primary focus like Ed does. Ed could do more reports, but he is focusing his business on homes more than ten years old. Ed has primarily limited his advertising to Google AdWords and his own newsletter. He hasn't even touched the new home market or tried home shows, seminars, direct mailing, talk shows, and the like. If he did, his company would grow to where he would need to hire additional energy auditors for the work load. For now, Ed is happy to have his strong six-digit income without employees.

To be an energy auditor you need to take a two-week class that costs around $450 and is offered online, and locally in some cities, by the Building Performance Institute (BPI - bpi.org). ResNet also offers courses and certification, but I reference BPI since that is who my friend Ed received his certification and training through. After the class, a 3-4 hour test must be passed along with some field tests. After passing the tests and with some basic equipment, you are ready to become an energy auditing professional. Here is what a typical energy audit consists of:

On Site Inspection:
- Meet with the homeowner to discuss the process.
- Measure the home like a realtor would.
- Determine the type, amount, and location of insulation.
- Inspect the doors, windows, seams, caulking, exterior, and any opening on the house.

- Inspect the appliances (gas stove, gas dryer) for efficiency.
- Inspect the furnace, water heater, and fireplace for safety, efficiency, and CO_2 emissions.
- Perform a Blower Door Test, which measures air leaks in a home.

Written Report:

With basic computer skills you can make the reports. There are "fill in the blank reports" you can easily create or purchase and customize for each customer. The energy audit report gives the results along with specific recommendations. Some energy auditors do the reports in the field while inspecting the home. My friend Ed's personal preference is to do the reports at his home office from his field notes. You can use color inks, photos, brochure paper, and folders to present the report in a professional way. Doing this will help the customer feel good about your services and advice and may just earn you referral business.

Follow-Up Visit:

After the report is completed most utility companies require you to explain the report in person to receive a reimbursement of the cost of the energy audit.

Potential Extra Income:

Homeowners often ask the auditors for recommendations on companies to perform the recommended work. Ed has been careful in this regard. He focuses on the audits as his business, not the potential work they generate. He wants to remain ethical in all of his recommendations and not base recommendations on what he could sell the homeowner. Ed doesn't mind helping the homeowner further, but only after he has fully explained the reasons for his recommendations, which prove that he is not making recommendations just to sell further services. He includes a "cost-benefit analysis" to show the investment and return of any work he recommends. This is very helpful for homeowners.

There is strong potential for extra income in the areas of minor handyman work and referral fees for larger jobs, such as a new furnace, windows, insulation, etc.

Some recommendations are minor such as increased weather stripping, caulking, and minor repairs. Ed has a handyman that is of great help to the homeowners requesting this service. Starting off, you could do the extra work yourself for extra income (around $35-$50/hour plus materials) or subcontract it to a handyman you know and trust. Be careful who you subcontract to as your reputation and livelihood are on the line.

Energy auditors have the ability to make strategic relationships with HVAC, insulation, roofing, and home improvement companies, which gets them preferred pricing and preferred scheduling for their customers as well as a referral fee for Ed. It is a win-win situation for all involved, but to remain ethical, the energy auditor should disclose to the homeowners that they do earn a referral fee for sending business. Because of the amount of business they refer, the pricing and service the homeowner will receive may be far better than if they contacted the firms on their own. In addition, the energy auditor should encourage the homeowner to get multiple bids.

At the end of this section in the Hypothetical Profit and Loss Statement, I make an estimate of what potential extra income could be. I intentionally estimated the extra income very low to be safe. Admittedly, this is a guess and your actual experience will vary.

ED'S STORY:
Ed had a good job working in sales and marketing until The Great Recession caused him to be downsized. In the meantime, he went to work for his friend's roofing company that wanted to add an insulation division. Ed was brought on to help launch the new insulation division. Ed had no experience in the building trades or with home construction.

Ed stumbled across energy audits when he found out that many insulation, HVAC, and home improvement companies were performing energy audits as a way to sell more business. In Ed's market area the local utility company provided rebates up to $2,000 for homeowners that added insulation after they had an energy audit. For many of the insulation, HVAC, and home improvement companies doing energy audits, their strategy was to sell more jobs based on the energy audits and rebates. In some cases grants were available, too. Most of these firms doing energy audits weren't as serious about energy audits as they were about their main business. Their customers often complained about the time it took to get many audit reports. Ed was concerned about the ethics of making energy saving recommendations while trying to up-sell them other services these companies performed.

In 2009, Ed launched his own energy audit firm after taking the two-week online course from BPI, doing field work, and passing the 2 - 3 hour test. All of this cost him $1,500 plus his time. The other equipment he needed for the business was an additional $5,000 or so, not counting his website, but including his business cards and forms. He already had a computer, smart phone, and reliable vehicle.

Ed started his business, relying heavily on Google AdWords to make sure his company appeared first in the search results for people looking for energy audits, energy savings, and more home comfort. In addition, Ed makes sure he contacts insulation companies, HVAC companies, and home improvement companies daily to network and build business for his company. Ed also offers customers a $25 gift card for referring business and he promotes his services regularly through his website and newsletter. Ed says he was profitable almost immediately.

Ed's Estimated Start-Up Costs: about $6,000 to $7,000. Your actual costs may vary, and you should verify this estimate for cost accuracy, and accuracy of the scope before investing funds or starting any venture.

Training, testing	$1,500 from BPI
Background Check	$100
Thermal Imaging gun	$1,500 to $2,500
Blower Door Testing equipment	$2,500
Ladder	$75
Notebook & Office supplies	$300
Business Cards	$65

Here is an example of the basic expected performance of an energy audit company. Your experience will vary based on your market, the amount of your extra income (if any) and the effort you put into it.

NOTE: This Profit and Loss Statement (also called a "P & L") is for discussion and informational purposes only. You should create your own P & L before investing funds or starting any new venture. You should not rely on this example to start your business from.

HYPOTHETICAL PROFIT AND LOSS STATEMENT

ESTIMATED MONTHLY INCOME

$8,000 Audit reports (assumes 4/week at a cost of $500 per report)

$800 Weatherization work

(Assumes $35/hour, 4 hour minimum, NOTE: the cost of materials are not factored as an expense below, as I assume the actual cost of all materials will be reimbursed by the homeowner)

$500 Referral fees (from insulation, HVAC, roofing, and home improvement companies that you send your clients too. You can negotiate special pricing for your clients, and still get a referral fee - making it a win-win for all involved)

$9,300 Total Estimated Gross Monthly Income

ESTIMATED MONTHLY EXPENSES

NOTE: this Estimate assumes you are investing cash, and not borrowing money. Therefore any interest expense you may have from borrowing money is not included herein, and should be included.

Business insurance	$100
Vehicle insurance	$100
Vehicle gas/oil	$400
Subcontracting	$190 (net after labor)
Internet expense	$75
Cell phone	$100
Advertising	$200
Office supplies	$200
Continuing education	$100
Office rent	FREE (if you work from your home)
Utilities	if any?
Business savings account	$500
Miscellaneous	$250

TOTAL ESTIMATED EXPENSES: **$2,215**

ESTIMATED NET INCOME, before taxes & debt service:

$7,085

SUCCESS SNAPSHOT

THE PUSHER

"Starting Is The Hardest Thing"

Big O, one of my friends from Leavenworth Federal Prison Camp, once told me that other than the big money he made (and spent) dealing drugs, the night life, the friends, and the adrenaline rush that came from being involved in that business were part of what appealed to him. When the heat is on, the glitz fades, the money is gone, and your "friends" don't return calls, it is then that you realize all you spent and risked left you empty and used. You know it's time for a change, which is why you are reading this book.

By now you realize you have legitimate business skills and have thought of ways you can use them to blast off into your new life. You're on the launch pad, and like the Space Shuttle, you have to push through with all your might and being. Making your new business work will be one of the hardest things you've ever done, yet it is still much easier than being in prison. You've hustled before; now go do it again--legitimately.

I've started many businesses for myself, partners, and clients. Do you want to know what the hardest part of starting a business is? It's **_STARTING_**. It has been said that what we do to avoid difficult things are usually worse than just doing them in the first place. I think some people stay in crime because they don't have a vision for another way to earn a living, or they don't make the effort to pursue their vision. Maybe you didn't know what to do to start a business, but now you do. You have the Business Plan Checklist™ and Success Snapshots to follow. If you need a business coach or consultant, we can help you through our website illegaltolegal.org.

Now go do whatever you can do to proceed forward no matter how small that may seem. Then keep on doing whatever you can do, and soon you will be blasting off to your new destiny!

The further the shuttle is away from the launch pad, the more momentum it gains and the easier it is to fly. That's one reason why you have to leave the criminal life behind and break away from the lifestyle that's holding you back. Doing a legal business won't always be hard. There comes a point when things start to click. Then your trouble isn't getting business, the trouble becomes managing your growth and success.

This Success Snapshot is the most important one in the book. This is *your* story. You must be "the Pusher." Push yourself to dream and envision your new life, push past your past, push yourself to plan, push past the people who doubt you or hold you back, and push past a lack of money. It may not be glamorous or glitzy, but it's so much better than the alternative. Push yourself to make a business and a life you can be proud of that won't leave you empty and destroyed.

I'll meet you at the launch pad. I believe in you. Your greatness is waiting for you to start.

> *"You don't have to be great to start,*
> *but you have to start to be great."*
>
> *-Zig Ziglar*

START BY:

1. Reading the Appendices in the back of this book. In them you will find:
   - A "user-friendly" version of the Business Plan Checklist™.
   - A sample business plan, and sample forms.
   - The full list of Pelshaw's Principles of Profitable Business.
   - Resources to help you in a job search.

2. Answering all of the questions in Chapters 1, 2, and 3.

3. Selecting a business to start that matches your strengths and passions.

4. Doing whatever you can legally do to blast off and make your dream a reality.

ACKNOWLEDGMENTS

Global leadership guru and best-selling author Dr. John C. Maxwell once said "one is too small of a number to achieve greatness." As it relates to this book nothing could be further from the truth. There were many people who helped make this project a reality, and who helped me through my forced "vacation" doing time at Leavenworth Federal Prison Camp.

To all the business owners who helped me with the Success Snapshot interviews–thank you for sharing your inspiring stories. To David McClendon: thank you for your ongoing friendship, patience, and prayers through the years. You have been a true brother and friend. To Vonda McEachern–The Vondanator--your cards, notes, emails, and other help meant the world to me while I was down, more than you will ever know. Kipp Colvin–talking to you is always an energizing joy–thank you for your friendship, and the books! Mike and Deb Terrell your friendship is a high point in my life–thanks for all you do and who you are. To Steve Willey: your faith in me, friendship, help, tolerance, and support have meant more to me than I could ever convey. More than once you have been a life saver, and you've always been an honorable gentleman, "my biggest fan," and a pleasure to be friends with. Steve, my brother Rich might fight you for the title of my biggest fan, as might Michael Pelshaw also: both of whom have my deep love and appreciation. To my "Sioux-ish" friend Arla Dillman: the two amigos rode again, and it was fun! Thanks for your edits, help, and friendship.

I want to thank "the fellas" at Leavenworth who helped me serve my time and helped with this book. Thank you for your input, involvement, and inspiration. Especially to Big O who so enthusiastically encouraged me to write and always kept me laughing, even if he didn't teach me his magic hot sauce recipe. To Derrick Taylor who read my scribble to me so I could quickly type the book on Trulinks. "Bishop" thank you for always keeping things interesting! Thank you Ron S. for your friendship, ethics, heart, input, and supporting the Equip lessons. To Ben and James: your stories helped get the ball rolling for the success snapshots. Ike: God will reward your heart and passion. Nick B., we have more great things to do when you are out, which we can do while speaking in a British accent! Wayne-O: you're a good man and a great friend. Fulton S.: "you da man" and I have deep respect for you. Will T.: thank you for your innovation, inspiration, and help. Mr. Goodwin, thank you for treating us like real human beings and making things more bearable. Mr. Hansen, thank you for really trying to make a difference. Darrell Smith thank you for helping me be grounded and balanced while doing time, as well as helping me get through. Thank you "Wingman" (Chris Campbell) for putting up with repeats of my same stories, for working out with me, and for being a friend.

Without the excellent preaching and ministry of Bishop T.D. Jakes I wouldn't have had the quote and concept to base this book on. My greatest thanks go to Ilaamen. For years she has stood by me through the storms and trials of life, which includes the writing of this book! Her passion, talent, and creativity are a precious treasure. Ilaamen I can't wait to spend the rest of my life with you. Your family is a treasure too! Especially your lovely parents and siblings.

PART THREE

APPENDICES

APPENDIX A
BUSINESS PLAN CHECKLIST™

Business Name:

Business Adress:

Business Owner(s) %

Contact Phone #:   Contact Email:

BUSINESS

- What is the need for this business?

- Have you Googled that name and checked with your Secretary of State to see if is available? if is available, register it with a Domain Registration Service like Go Daddy (Should cost about $10)

- Have you registered the business name with your Secretary of State as soon as you can so no one else uses it.

- Why do you want to be in this business?

- Will you start this business from scratch, buy an existing business, or buy a franchise for this business?

- What licensing, training, or experience do you need for this? If more is needed, how can you get it/them?

- What is your work experience?

- What is your experience in this business, if any?

- Do you need to work for a company in this field before starting your own business doing this, or can you learn as you go?

- What do you believe your strengths in this business will be?

- Do you have a specialty or a niche you can serve, if so, what?

- Who is your competition?

- Where are they located?

- What does your competition do well?

- What does your competition do poorly?

- What will make you unique or better than competition?

- What is your "elevator speech?"

- Have you made a map of your city which includes the location of your competition plus the location of any businesses that can be a positive or negative influence for you?

- Is the market underserved or saturated? Why do you think that?

- What is the target geographical area you will start serving? Expand to?

- What are the geographic limits of your service territory?

- What is your mission with your business, other than making money?

- Do you have anyone you can get to mentor you in your new venture?

- Who are your vendors and suppliers?

- What will you need to do to establish credit with them, and under what terms?

- What is your plan for the first 3 months?

- What is your plan for the first year?

- What is your plan for the second year?

CUSTOMERS

- Who are your target customers? Why did you choose this group?

- How will you relate to or be relevant to this group?

- What are the demographics of your target customer? Are they above, below, or at the average for your target geographic area?

- How will you reach your customers?

- How much will you spend on your initial advertising and promotions?

- How will you advertise and promote your business?

- Will you, or how will you, use "social media?"

- Do you know what the expected response rate of your proposed advertising is?

- What is your competition doing to advertise and promote?

- Will you offer a coupon, special, or other promotion? If so what?

PRODUCTS & SERVICES

- What is the cost and price of your product(s) or service(s)?

- How did you determine the cost and price?

- What is your starting inventory of product, if any?

- How does your product mix, inventory, and proposed prices compare with your competition?

- Do you need any licenses or permits to work in this area?

- Do you need to collect sales tax on your goods and services?

- Do you need a logo?

- Do you need a website?

- Who will do your website if you have one?

- Will you do sales over the internet?

- Who will process your payments?

- Will you do your own order fulfillment, if any?

ADMINISTRATIVE, STAFFING, OWNERSHIP

- When/where can you get business cards at?

- Where will you do your banking at? Why?

- Do you need to accept credit cards? If so, who will you use?

- How many employees do you need? How much will you pay them?

- What are the job positions, and how many of each, do you need to fill to function?

- How do you intend to operate the business?

- Is it just you, or will you hire managers? Do you have family members to help out?

- How will train and supervise your team?

- Will you use subcontractors, if so, where and how?

- Can you operate your business from home or do you need to rent a shop, store, or office space?

- How much space to you need for your business?

- Do you have a good commercial real estate agent to help you?

- Do you need to maintain a service department? If so what do you need for facilities, equipment, staff, and supplies to operate it?

- What are you doing to provide customer service?

- How will it be owned? Will you incorporate, make an LLC (limited liability company), or a partnership?

- Who all will own the business (list percentages ownership and responsibilities of any partners)

- If it is a corporation, who are the officers?

- What is the "chain of command?"

FURNITURE, FIXTURES, & EQUIPMENT (FF&E)

- What equipment, tools, computers, vehicles, and furniture do you need to have?

- Where can you buy them?

- Can you buy them used for less than new?
- What will each item cost? Is there a monthly payment associated with them?

- How will you pay for them? (A loan, Personal funds, Money from a partner, or investor?)

- Will you lease or rent them? Can you get these items on a payment plan, or with delayed payment, and pay for them from the operation of your new business?

INSURANCE and LEGAL

- How much will your insurance cost?

- Who is your insurance company and what is the policy number?

- Do you have an attorney? *(Name / Phone Number / Email)*

FINANCIAL

- **Tax ID #:** *(www.irs.gov has these for free. Search "Employer ID numbers". They also have links to each State Tax ID #s)*

- Do you have a CPA or bookkeeper? *(Name / Phone Number / Email)*

- Who will maintain your financial records? *(Name / Phone Number / Email)*

- Who will handle your finances? *(Name / Phone Number / Email)*

- What are your start-up costs?

- What can you do to raise money, if needed? Do you have friends, family, a bank or an investor you can approach?

- How much have you budgeted for start-up?

ESTIMATED START-UP LIST

- Payroll
- Contract labor
- Rent
- Utilities
- Internet
- Cell phones and telephones
- Website
- Insurance
- Bonding costs
- Banking expense
- Bookkeeping expense
- Vehicle expense
- Payroll taxes
- Income taxes
- Debt service and/or lease payments
- Supplies
- Materials
- Inventory
- Repairs
- Shipping
- Travel
- Commissions
- Marketing
- Collection loss
- Legal/professional fees
- Franchise fees or license fees
- Savings and reserves
- Any additional items?

+ _____ **TOTAL**

- How much of the Start-Up Cost do you have now?

- If there is a deficit what is your plan to fund it?

- What is your overhead, monthly and annually?

- How much business do you realistically project you can do in the first 3 months? 6 months? Year? 2 Years?

- How did you determine the future income?

FIRST YEAR

	Month 1	Month 2	Month 3	Month 4	Month 5	Month 6	Month 7	Month 8	Month 9	Month 10	Month 11	Month 12	Total
INCOME													
Sales Income													
Service Income													
Other Income													
TOTAL INCOME													
EXPENSES													
Payroll													
Contract labor													
Rent													
Utilities													
Internet													
Cell phone/telephones													
Website													
Insurance													
Bonding costs													
Banking expense													
Bookkeeping expense													
Vehicle expense													
Payroll taxes													
Income taxes													
Debt service/lease Pmts													
Supplies													
Materials													
Inventory													
Repairs													
Shipping													
Travel													
Commissions													
Marketing													
Collection loss													
Legal/professional fees													
Franchise/license fees													
Savings and reserves													
Other													
TOTAL EXPENSES													

SECOND YEAR

	Month 1	Month 2	Month 3	Month 4	Month 5	Month 6	Month 7	Month 8	Month 9	Month 10	Month 11	Month 12	Total
INCOME													
Sales Income													
Service Income													
Other Income													
TOTAL INCOME													
EXPENSES													
Payroll													
Contract labor													
Rent													
Utilities													
Internet													
Cell phone/telephones													
Website													
Insurance													
Bonding costs													
Banking expense													
Bookkeeping expense													
Vehicle expense													
Payroll taxes													
Income taxes													
Debt service/lease Pmts													
Supplies													
Materials													
Inventory													
Repairs													
Shipping													
Travel													
Commissions													
Marketing													
Collection loss													
Legal/professional fees													
Franchise/license fees													
Savings and reserves													
Other													
TOTAL EXPENSES													

Notes and Assumptions:

- Given all of these factors and costs, what is "break even point."

- How long does it take you to get to your break-even point?

- What is your projected cash shortage during your first 12 months of operation? What is your plan to deal with it?

- Is there a projected cash shortage during your second 12 months of operation? What is your plan to deal with it?

MISCELLANEOUS

- List any special circumstances, to do items, or issues to deal with here:

APPENDIX B

SAMPLE BUSINESS PLAN

I wrote this as an actual business plan, and changed some names to make this sample for you. This is a very short business plan, but it tells the story of what we were trying to do. Note the financial projections at the end of this plan. Enjoy!

TBTV Sample Business Plan

Thrift Stores have always been a highly profitable business venture, but until now, they have not been a top-shelf part of main stream retailing. Thrift stores in the past have been little more than "junk shops" mostly owned by non-profits without retail expertise, and operated with volunteer staff that sometimes lacked the professionalism, passion, and training of a serious career retailer. National chains like Goodwill, with over $3 Billion in sales, have shown that thrift stores are not only a major retailing segment, but they have increased the profile and improved the way thrift stores are retailing. They have done this by using their management and operational systems to make higher-end free standing stores in neighborhoods not traditionally associated with upscale thrift stores. The Salvation Army also operates a national network of thrift stores, but in my opinion they are behind Goodwill in the more upscale positioning of their store brand.

The thrift, vintage, and used material industries have proven that retailers selling used wares can thrive nationally if approached with the same proper metrics as other national retail ventures, such as: the right location, co-tenant mix, proper customer profile, effective brand creation, and effective management.

The Great Recession has changed consumer preferences so that thrift stores, often referred to as "shabby sheik" or "vintage" have a panache or cool/acceptability factor not previously experienced in this industry. Where once shopping at a thrift store was something only the lowest demographic groups did, popular shows like *American Pickers, Road Show Antiques*, and *Pawn Stars* have enlivened the American consumer to the point that an emerging shopping segment of consumers hunting for antiques, cool vintage deals, and basic everyday bargains has been created. Many realize shopping at thrift and vintage stores is a fun and often rewarding past time. Finally, The Green Movements have educated consumers on the benefits on recycling, adding an additional customer base now fiercely loyal to thrift and vintage shopping. This target customer group is better educated, has more disposal income, and shops more frequently than the previous traditional thrift store consumer.

Thrift/vintage is not just for clothing – antique hounds, decorators, and higher income shoppers regularly frequent these establishments looking for unique and cool pieces. Because of the Great Recession, those hunting for vintage and antique items, and the Green Movement, consumer preferences have fundamentally changed and evolved into a higher demand, higher relevance, and higher acceptability of those thrift and vintage operations that target the savvy, more trendy, and more cost conscious higher demographic consumer. Because of the changing nature of inventory, loyal customers shop frequently.

Currently there are no for-profit national upscale for-profit thrift/vintage operations capitalizing on this shift in consumer preferences. The goal of TBTV is to operate its store in a way to build a system that can be profitably franchised nationally, and use the profits from the stores to acquire the buildings/shopping centers TBTV stores are located in. According to industry sources, on a national average thrift stores have annual sales per square foot in the $40-$100/SF range. Vintage store sales can be $60-$300 per square foot, according to these same sources.

We believe there is substantial opportunity for a highly profitable national chain of thrift/vintage stores that is properly positioned to target the traditional thrift store consumer while attracting the thrift/vintage shopper, the bargain hunter, and the green consumer.

The key to a thrift/vintage store is a great location relative to target customer groups and competition. The Great Recession has created an abundance of prime retail stores, often in shopping centers and buildings that are financially distressed, bank-owned, or with an otherwise highly motivated landlord – all of whom could be potential sellers of real estate at bargain-basement prices. We propose to expand as warranted, and where possible and feasible, use the lease and operating profits to profitably acquire the buildings and/or shopping centers that our stores open in.

A well respected thrift/vintage operation is **BITD** owned by John Doe. They have two locations, one at 123 Main Street and the other at Old Town Center. **BITD** has these successful locations and a loyal following of the higher demographic vintage customer, as well as loyal thrift customers.

In its current location on Main Street *BITD* has averaged sales of over $65/SF, which has considerable obstacles to retailing. The second location has higher sales. The Main Street store has less than 3,000 SF of sales space, on 3 different levels, has no off street parking, is mid-block, and does not have any major customer traffic generators like a grocery store or dollar store, yet it is still averaging $15,000/month in gross sales.

A large part of *BITD's* success is that they have specialized in thematic departments, almost mini-boutiques inside their store, such as Vinyl, Retro, and then by decade or period (such as 50's, 60's, etc.). Each department is operated by an assistant. Since this area is becoming known as an artist community, is enroute to downtown, and this trade area is already established for *BITD*.

BITD has gained a reputation for buying bulk Estates, and general for sale items, often buying items for a small fraction of what it would sell for in the store. Often there are excess items acquired in this process that once sorted by *BITD* it's determined those items should not be sold in the Vintage store. Currently a large amount of good salable items are donated to area thrift stores. Mr. Doe wishes to launch TBTV to be a thrift store exploiting the current retail environment while utilizing excess inventory acquired from *BITD* .

TBTV was birthed from the two successful vintage stores of *BITD*. Mr. Doe has over 30 years successful thrift and vintage business operations experience. *BITD* has over 1,000,000 thrift and vintage items stored at various warehouses, which will be part of the initial and ongoing inventory for TBTV. TBTV will benefit from the inventory *BITD* acquires but doesn't sell in their stores. *BITD* will promote TBTV to its customer base. We are excited to say that TBTV has entered into an agreement with Big Brothers Big Sisters to be their exclusive Thrift Store Partner, which allows us direct access to their database, the ability to offer tax deductible receipts for donations, and the ability to say "a portion of proceeds will be donated to Big Brothers Big Sisters."

The first TBTV is a proposed thrift store to be located at "S Plaza" in a 6,700 SF retail bay at 2910 K Street Suite B, Anywhere, TX, in the heart of a Latino neighborhood. S Plaza is anchored by Aldi's Grocery Store, Dollar Tree, Aaron's Rent to Own, and Little Caesar's Pizza. These are fantastic high traffic well recognized co-tenants for a thrift/vintage store.

Each operation at S Plaza reports brisk sales and S Plaza has become a community center on the L Street Corridor. "L" Street is the retail and commercial epicenter of Anywhere TX, intersecting with 24th East about a half mile east. Between S Plaza and 24th Street is US Highway 5, which is a major north/south commuter corridor. West of S Plaza is Big Plaza, which is a Hy-Vee anchored grocery center with great success.

Over 80,000 adults reside within 3 miles of S Plaza, making it one of the most densely populated areas in the state. There is a high blue collar demographic, one that is very appropriate for the tenant mix and target customer of S Plaza and TBTV. This neighborhood has traditionally been known as a thrift store trade area, and with economic conditions and a resurgence of interest in vintage items, Thrift Stores are a highly lucrative business segment. Please see Appendix D for a demographic profile.

5 Year Projected P&L

	$44/SF ann. sales	$70/SF ann. sales	$80/SF ann. sales	$85/SF ann. sales	$89/SF ann. sales	$94/SF ann. sales
INCOME	2013	2014	2015	2016	2017	2018
Gross Sales	$297,500	$469,000	$536,000	$569,500	$597,975	$627,874
EXPENSES						
Cost of Goods Sold	$55,500	$35,000	$40,000	$42,000	$44,000	$46,000
Advertising	$22,000	$24,000	$24,000	$25,000	$25,000	$26,000
Communication Expense (Phone, internet, website)	$4,200	$4,500	$4,500	$4,800	$4,800	$5,100
Merchant Services -3%	$8,925	$14,070	$16,080	$17,085	$17,939	$18,836
Rent - Store ($5/SF 1ST YEAR, 3% annual increases)	$19,542	$20,128	$20,732	$21,354	$21,995	$22,655
Rent - Warehouse behind store ($2/SF 1st yr. w/3% ann inc)	$5,495	$5,660	$5,830	$6,005	$6,185	$6,370
Utilities (store & warehouse)	$12,400	$12,800	$13,250	$13,600	$13,900	$14,200
Taxes - Real Estate ($1/SF for 11,400 SF)	$11,400	$11,400	$11,400	$11,400	$11,400	$11,400
Insurance - Property Casualty & Liability	$3,600	$3,700	$3,700	$3,800	$3,800	$3,800
Maintenance - Property (CAM - $1/SF for 11,400 SF)	$11,400	$11,400	$11,650	$11,650	$11,800	$12,000
Transportation - Inventory	$27,500	$30,000	$32,500	$35,000	$37,500	$40,000
Payroll (4 PT staff 30 hr./wk. @$8 hr. salary + $2/hr. taxes/bnfts)	$68,370	$75,000	$80,000	$85,000	$90,000	$95,000
Administrative (outsource bookkeeping and accounting)	$12,000	$12,500	$13,000	$13,500	$14,000	$15,000
Charitable Split (5% gross sales)	$14,875	$23,450	$26,800	$28,475	$29,899	$31,394
Total Expenses	$277,207	$283,608	$303,442	$318,669	$332,217	$347,755
NET EARNINGS	$20,293	$185,392	$232,558	$250,831	$265,758	$280,119

We believe these projections are conservative, and do not factor economies of scale from existing store operations and expansions. We anticipate being able to open the store with a $50,000 capital investment. Capital investment and return will be repaid from net earnings.

From an investment standpoint, *TBTV* is an attractive opportunity with a unique business model that capitalizes on trends in the economy, consumer preference, retail real estate, and that can hopefully grow through franchise and organic expansion into a national chain.

Thank you for your consideration.

APPENDIX C: SAMPLE FORMS

TBTV Thrift Store
Profit and Loss Statement
January – June 20xx

	Jan - Jun 20xx
Ordinary Income/Expense	
Income	
Gross Sales	297,500
Less: Cost of Goods sold	-55,500
Gross Profit	242,000
Expense	
Advertising and Promotion	22,000
Communication	4,200
Merchant Services	8,925
Rent: Store	19,542
Rent: Warehouse	5,495
Utilities	12,400
Real Estate Taxes	11,400
Insurance	3,600
Maintenance: Property	11,400
Transportation: Inventory	27,500
Payroll (inc. payroll taxes)	68,370
Administrative	12,000
Charitable split	14,875
Total Expense	271,707
Net Income	20,293

When you make your own Profit & Loss Statement (also known as a "P&L" or an "Income Statement") you can add or subtract income or expense categories as you need it. When you mark receipts for your business go ahead and mark the expense category right on the expense. For instance, if you pay your gas bill, before you put that receipt in your wallet or file write on the receipt "Utilities" so that when you or the bookkeeper goes to input that expense they automatically know which category to put it in. More on using P&L's in the next sample form.

APPENDIX C: SAMPLE FORMS

TBTV Thrift Store
Balance Sheet
January – June 20xx

ASSETS

    Current Assets

        Checking/Savings

Checking	73,967.86
Total Checking/Savings	73,967.86
Accounts Receivable	
Inventory	99,530.32
Total Accounts Receivable	99,530.32
Total Current Assets	173,498.18
Fixed Assets	
Furniture and Equipment	12,000.00
Total Fixed Assets	12,000.00
TOTAL ASSETS	**185,498.18**

LIABILITIES & EQUITY

    Liabilities

Credit Cards	1,000.00
Accounts Payable	73,678.85
Total Current Liabilities	74,678.85
Total Liabilities	74,678.85
Equity	
Retained Earnings	100.00
Shareholder Distributions	-1,333.00
Net Income	112,052.33
Total Equity	110,819.33
TOTAL LIABILITIES & EQUITY	**185,498.18**

Bankers, CPAs, and investors like balance sheets. A balance sheet is supposed to be a snapshot of the overall financial condition of a business. A P&L will give you a snapshot of the profitability of a business. Use them together for a complete picture of a company.

APPENDIX C

SAMPLE FORMS INVOICE OR PROPOSAL

Your Company, Inc. INVOICE

Address
City, State, ZIP   (555) 555-555

SOLD TO:
Name
Address
City, State, ZIP

INVOICE NUMBER	536524
INVOICE DATE	August 2, 2014
OUR ORDER NO.	726278
YOUR ORDER NO.	1892727
TERMS	Net 30
SALES REP	Name
SHIPPED VIA	Air
F.O.B.	City, State
PREPAID or COLLECT	COLL

SHIPPED TO:
Same

Sales Tax Rate: 5.00%

QUANTITY	DESCRIPTION	UNIT PRICE	AMOUNT
120	Product	10.00	$1,200.00
120	Product	10.00	1,200.00

TERMS: 2%/net 10. Interest of 1.5% per month on all past due amounts.

SUBTOTAL	2,400.00
TAX	120.00
FREIGHT	
PAY THIS AMOUNT	$2,520.00

DIRECT ALL INQUIRIES TO:
Name
(555) 555-555
email: someone@somename.com

MAKE ALL CHECKS PAYABLE TO:
Your Company, Inc.
Attn: Accounts Receivable
Address
City, State, ZIP

THANK YOU FOR YOUR BUSINESS!

This invoice was printed from an un-copyrighted template in Microsoft Excel. You can create invoices and proposals from both Excel and QuickBooks, and other programs as well. Make this invoice into a proposal by detailing the work to be done and including a place for customers to sign and accept your proposal. You can find an invoice or proposal template online at Google by searching for "free sample invoice" or " free proposal forms." Beware of services wanting you to subscribe to something to get free forms. Avoid those and check others.

APPENDIX D

SAMPLE DEMOGRAPHIC REPORT FOR TBTV

Population	1-mi.	3-mi.	5-mi.
2013 Male Population	8,980	55,340	119,992
2013 Female Population	8,519	52,467	119,610
% 2013 Male Population	51.32%	51.33%	50.08%
% 2013 Female Population	48.68%	48.67%	49.92%
2013 Total Population: Adult	12,190	80,387	178,848
2013 Total Daytime Population	16,312	167,002	323,461
2013 Total Employees	6,039	107,632	193,144
2013 Total Population: Median Age	30	30	32
2013 Total Population: Adult Median Age	41	40	43
Housing	**1-mi.**	**3-mi.**	**5-mi.**
2000 Housing Units	6,684	46,458	100,567
2000 Occupied Housing Units	6,170	42,825	93,977
2000 Owner Occupied Housing Units	3,269	20,713	53,658
2000 Renter Occupied Housing Units	2,901	22,112	40,319
2000 Vacant Housings Units	514	3,633	6,590
% 2000 Occupied Housing Units	92.31%	92.18%	93.45%
% 2000 Owner occupied housing units	52.98%	48.37%	57.10%
% 2000 Renter occupied housing units	47.02%	51.63%	42.90%
% 2000 Vacant housing units	7.69%	7.82%	6.55%
Income	**1-mi.**	**3-mi.**	**5-mi.**
2013 Median Household Income for the County	$48,147	$48,147	$48,147
2013 Household Income: Median	$33,082	$36,862	$39,422
2013 Household Income: Average	$40,936	$46,237	$50,366
2013 Per Capita Income	$13,926	$18,382	$20,002
2013 Median Per Capita Income for the County	$27,546	$27,546	$27,546

Please note: This is an excerpt of a much larger demographic report. A complete demographic report can contain a breakdown of the population by age, and show if that population has increased or decreased over time. It can also show the potential retail or service sales in an area, the ethnic breakdown of an area, how many people own or rent their homes, what their education level is, and more.

I know it looks like a lot of boring information, but if you take the time to look one over, and ask the right questions, a demographic report can show you markets that are goldmines, or dry holes to avoid.

When you look at a demographic report ask yourself two questions:
1). How does the person this report profiles compare to the customer I want? 2). How does the person this report profiles compare to the average in my community? For instance, I look at the total population within an area, their income, and how that compares to the median household or per capita income for that city or county. That tells me if I am in a low or high income area. Changes in the population over time will tell me if the area is growing or stagnating. Above you can see that the median per capita income is half of what the county average is, so this is a low-income area. You can see it's a younger population with a lot of people, the majority of whom rent. Can a well-run thrift store thrive there?

APPENDIX E

PELSHAW'S PRINCIPLES OF PROFITABLE BUSINESS

1. Everything must pay for itself. Make your operations, management, and back office direct enough and focused enough so that you can always determine whether a business activity is in fact paying for itself or not. Use this rule to also help you keep the emotions out of the tough decisions.

2. Make money by solving problems.

3. Never let the kids control the daycare, but be humble enough and have enough leadership to develop your people and let them excel in their jobs, careers, and lives.

4. Never get involved in anything you can't control unless you trust that person or organization with more than just your money.

5. Never get involved in anything operationally intensive unless you are willing to be involved in the operations.

6. Never get involved in anything you don't understand, and keep it simple so the vision and goals are always clear and measurable.

7. Always focus on strengths by using the 80/20 rule (also known as the Paretto Principal) then delegate or staff areas of your weakness(es).

8. Always do what you say you are going to do, and always "under promise" and "over achieve."

9. Leaders aren't paid to take risks; we are paid to know and implement those risks which are worth taking.

10. The Golden Rule: Treat others as you want to be treated.

11. Treat the cleaning lady with the same respect you treat a CEO.

12. Never let anything good done to you ever go without expressing gratitude or appreciation, no matter how small.

13. Never bid against yourself.

14. Don't drag someone to the altar – always strive for "buy in."

15. Never have a meeting without an agenda or knowing in advance what you are supposed to accomplish.

16. Never bring up a problem without several good solutions.

17. Make your money on the "Buy" by buying at the best price possible.

18. Pigs get Fat, but Hogs get Slaughtered – never be greedy.

19. Everybody has to make money – the deal must be good for everyone if it is to get done. Strive for everyone to be "happy but not ecstatic".

20. To have 51 percent ownership in a venture is nice for control of the organization, but never be partners with someone, or hire someone, you have to have control over, or always need to look over your shoulder at them.

21. Get out of the way of the best people and empower them to do their work.

22. Hire slowly, fire quickly (from Jack Welch, former CEO of General Electric).

23. Know what business you're in and why.

24. Have the best system, look at McDonald's, they don't have the best hamburger but they are the most successful because they have the best and most consistent system. (from Robert Kiyosaki).

25. All marketing is personal. Don't leave it on auto-pilot through your website, social media, and online means, but have a great purple, powerful elevator speech, and remember your selling to individuals.

26. Never do a deal unless you have a short term and a long term exit strategy, and those strategies make sense.

27. Never be emotionally attached to any deal – this is defined by the fact that you should be able to walk away from any deal at any time.

28. Observe in total reality but always deal in hope (from Peter Drucker).

29. Stay under the radar so you don't get shot down.

30. All marketing is personal, even if you are using online resources.

31. Never let your pride and ego get in the way of your judgment and view of reality. Never believe your own press reports or have "candidate-itis," or "bigshotitis."

32. Get the right people on the bus, and give them authority to take the bus where it needs to go. I define authority as giving away enough responsibility for people to make their own mistakes or successes.

33. Remember that the same success that got you where you are is not the same success you will need to maintain your current position, or the same success you will need to go to the next level. (John Maxwell).

34. Reinvent yourself every five years (from John Maxwell).

35. If you don't like the game, change the rules.

36. Be Development oriented, not Growth oriented. If you focus on developing, growth will take care of itself (from John Maxwell).

37. Serve People and use Things, NEVER serve Things and use People.

38. Every day add value to the people and projects you touch.

39. Every day justify the reasons why you consumed air.

■■

PELSHAW'S INVESTING PRINCIPLES:

1. I never invest in anything I don't understand.
2. I never invest in anything I don't control unless I trust the other parties so much that I don't have to control it.
3. The return OF money is more important than return ON money.
4. Create cash flow by solving problems, and invest the cash flow to create more wealth.
5. Know your strengths and weaknesses, and always focus on your strengths.
6. I try to achieve a five-year payback minimum for any investment unless it is a very safe conservative investment.
7. Make money by exploiting opportunities created by solving problems.
8. Make your money on the "Buy" by buying something for the best price possible.

APPENDIX F

LIST OF BOOKS
TO PRISONERS PROGRAMS

Many inmates are voracious readers, and the following is a list of organizations that provide inmates free books. If you are an inmate, you can mail a request to them for a free book by giving them the top five types of books or authors you want, and they will do their best to provide you a book as close as possible to your request.

The list below is most of the "books to prisoner programs" in the United States that we know of. The list will provide the contact information for sending a book request, and the service area of the organization. Special information about specific programs, if any, is provided after the area of service. For a current list of Books to Prisoners Programs please check out this website (which is the sources of this list):

prisonbookprogram.org/resources/other-books-to-prisoners-programs/

These groups need your support to continue to help prisoners. If you have books to donate, or can help with funds so they can ship books to inmates, any of the groups on this list would be a great place to invest your charitable contributions.

To support these critically needed programs we regularly provide free copies of ILLEGAL TO LEGAL to "books to prisoner programs" that request them, and we also sell them books at cost. If you have a "books to prisoner program" that should be listed here, if you need to update contact information, or request copies of ILLEGAL TO LEGAL for your program please contact us at info@illegaltolegal.org.

I hope this list is useful for you!

ASHEVILLE PRISON BOOKS PROGRAM
67 N Lexington Ave
Asheville, NC 28801
prisonbooks31@hotmail.com
http://www.main.nc.us/prisonbooks
(Serves NC, SC, GA, and TN)

ATHENS BOOKS TO PRISONERS
30 1st Street
Athens, OH 45701
athensbooks2prisoners@gmail.com
www.facebook.com/athensbookstoprisoners   (Serves Ohio)

APPALACHIAN PRISON BOOK PROJECT
PO Box 601
Morgantown, WV 26507
appalachianpbp@gmail.com
https://aprisonbookproject.wordpress.com/
(Serves KY, MD, OH, TN, VA, WV)

BELLINGHAM BOOKS TO PRISONERS
c/o Left Bank Books
92 Pike Street, Box A
Seattle, WA 98101
http://www.bellinghambtp.org/
info@bellinghambtp.org
(Serves All USA ex. CA and MA)

BOOK 'EM
5129 Penn Ave.
Pittsburgh, PA 15224
http://www.bookempgh.org/
bookempgh@gmail.com
(Serves Pennsylvania only)

BOOKS BETWEEN THE BARS
2309 Apollo Road Box 605
Garland, Texas 75044
http://booksbetweenthebars.webs.com/
(Serves Texas only) You can request a book every 60 days, but be specific on the types of books you request.

BOOKS THROUGH BARS – NYC
c/o Bluestockings
172 Allen St
New York, NY 10002
booksthroughbarsnyc.org
(Serves all of the USA)

BOOKS THROUGH BARS, PHILADELPHIA
4722 Baltimore Ave
Philadelphia, PA 19143
http://booksthroughbars.org/
info@booksthroughbars.org
(Serves PA, NJ, NY, DE, MD, VA, and WV)

BOOKS TO PRISONERS - SEATTLE
c/o Left Bank Books
92 Pike Street, Box A
Seattle, WA 98101
http://www.bookstoprisoners.net/
bookstoprisoners@live.com
(Serves: All US states except CA and MA) You can request books once every nine months.

CHICAGO BOOKS TO WOMEN IN PRISON
Chicago Books to Women in Prison
c/o RFUMC
4511 N. Hermitage Ave.
Chicago, IL 60640
http://chicagobwp.org/
chicagobwp@gmail.com
(Serves AZ, CA, CT, FL, IL, IN, KY, MS, MO, and OH)

DC BOOKS TO PRISONS
PO Box 34190
Washington, DC 20043-4190
http://dcbookstoprisoners.org/
btopdc@gmail.com
(Serves All US States except New England, IL, NJ, NY, OH, OR, PA, WA, WI.)

GAINESVILLE BOOKS FOR PRISONERS
P.O. Box 12164
Gainesville, FL 32604
www.civicmediacenter.org/links/2003/11/01/13.29.05.htm
(Serves all of the USA)
Accepts requests by topic only.

INSIDE BOOKS PROJECT
c/o 12th Street Books
827 West 12th Street
Austin, Texas 78701
http://insidebooksproject.org
insidebooksproject@gmail.com
(Serves TX only)

INTERNATIONALIST PRISON BOOK COLLECTIVE
http://prisonbooks.info/
prisonbooks@gmail.com
(Serves AL, some prisons in NC)

BOOKS THRU BARS OF ITHACA
c/o Autumn Leaves Used Books
115 The Commons
Ithaca, NY 14850
www.booksthrubars.org (NY only)

BOOKS 2 PRISONERS
831 Elysian Fields Box# 143
New Orleans, LA 70117
books2prisoners@gmail.com
(Serves AL, AR, LA, MS.)

MIDWEST PAGES TO PRISONERS PROJECT
c/o Boxcar Books
310A S. Washington St.
Bloomington, IN 47401
(AR, IN, IA, KS, KY, MN, MO, NE, ND, OH, OK, SD, TN, & WI)

OLYMPIA BOOKS TO PRISONERS
c/o Center for Community Based Learning and Action
The Evergreen State College,
 Sem II E2125,
2700 Evergreen Pkwy NW
Olympia, WA 98505
http://olympiabtp.org/
olybtp@gmail.com
(Serves entire USA)

OPEN BOOKS BOOKSTORE +PRISON BOOK PROJECT
1040 N. Guillemard St.
Pensacola, FL 32501
www.openbookspcola.org
(Serves Florida only)

PORTLAND BOOKS TO PRISONERS
c/o Left Bank Books
92 Pike Street. Box A
Seattle, WA 98101
portland.indymedia.org/en/2003/06/265772.shtml
(Serves All US states except MA)
Request by topic not author. No legal or religious requests.

PRISON BOOK PROGRAM
1306 Hancock St. Suite 100
Quincy, MA 02169
www.prisonbookprogram.org/
(Serves all states but CA, MA, MD, MI, PA, or TX).

PRISON BOOK PROJECT
c/o Food for Thought Books
P.O. Box 396
Amherst, MA 01004-0396
www.prisonbooks.org
(Serves All US states except MA)

PRISONER LITERATURE PROJECT
c/o Bound Together Books
1369 Haight St.
San Francisco, CA 94117
(Serves All US states except OR and MA)

PROVIDENCE BOOKS THROUGH BARS
c/o Atlas Bower Books
245 Meeting Street
Providence, RI 02906
prov_booksthroughbars@yahoo.org
(Serves all USA)

READ BETWEEN THE BARS
c/o Daily Planet Publishing
P.O. Box 1589
Tucson, AZ 85702-1589
http://readbetweenthebars.com/
readbetweenthebars@gmail.com
(Serves AZ only)

READING REDUCES RECIDIVISM
http://www.3rsproject.org
Serves prison libraries in Illinois and does not ship books to prisoners.

URBANA-CHAMPAIGN BOOKS TO PRISONERS PROJECT
UC Books to Prisoners
Box 515 Urbana IL 61803
http://www.books2prisoners.org/
(Serves Illinois)

UNITARIAN UNIVERSALIST ANN ARBOR PRISON BOOKS
prisonbooks@uuaa.org
http://uuaa.org/index.php/social-justice/faith-in-action/prison-books
(Serves Select Michigan)

WISCONSIN BOOKS TO PRISONERS
c/o Rainbow Bookstore
426 W. Gilman Street
Madison, WI 53703
https://www.prisonactivist.org/resources/wisconsin-books-prisoners-project
wisconsinbookstoprisoners@yahoo.com
(Serves Wisconsin only)

WOMEN'S PRISON BOOK PROJECT
c/o Boneshaker Books
2002 23rd Ave S
Minneapolis, MN 55404
(Serves All US states except CT, FL, IL, IN, MA, MI, MS, OH, OR, and PA)

APPENDIX G

This is a tool for you to use to help your job searches. For more information about the National Hire Ex - Felons Campaign, and for more free resources, please visit illegaltolegal.org.

 ## TEN BOTTOM-LINE REASONS TO HIRE EX-FELONS

brought to you by **The National Hire Ex-Felons Campaign and illegaltolegal.org**

We don't want to appeal to your humanitarian side and play the "everyone deserves a second chance" card. Instead here are ten fact-based, bottom-line enhancing, benefits of hiring felons.

1. Show me the money! Substantial tax credits are available for hiring felons. The programs are very easy to use without a lot of red tape. Check this site for the Federal Work Opportunity Tax Credit doleta.gov/wotc. Some states even provide partial wage reimbursement, additional tax credits, and other training funds for employers that hire felons. Check your local state's Department of Revenue and Workforce Development Office for programs where you live. "We've had three (subsidies) that amounts to several hundreds of thousands of dollars to bear down on training our employees. It's amazing to me how many resources are available to company, but they don't take the time to go after them." Mike Hannigan, CEO of Give Something Back.

2. I need some assurances. How about some free insurance for you? Employers that hire felons can be eligible to obtain a free fidelity bond funded by the Federal government to protect you against employee dishonesty or theft. Look for the contact in your state at bonds4jobs.com. More importantly, credible studies clearly indicate that ex-felons out of prison seven years or more have no higher rate of committing a crime than non-felons. Kiminori Nakamura, assistant professor at the University of Maryland, co-authored a 2009 study that found people with a criminal record are at no greater criminal risk after they've been out seven to 10 years than those with no record. "Very old criminal records are not very useful in predicting risk," he said.

3. Does that come with a guarantee? Yep – especially if someone is on probation. Ex-offenders on probation often have to keep a job and perform well at work as a condition of their release. Most parolees are drug-tested by their probation officer or halfway house at no expense to you. Most parole officers and halfway houses welcome contact with employers of supervised felons. They will refer you more workers if you let them know the type of person you want to hire. *A parole officer supervising a felon you employ = added value at no cost to you*! An estimated 6,899,000 persons were under the supervision of adult correctional systems in 2013, according to the Bureau of Justice. This is a significant, largely untapped and motivated work force.

4. What's the turnover rate? Due to the scarcity of opportunities for felons, many employers that hire felons have lower turnover than with conventional hires. As mentioned, parole officers and halfway houses can be a great source of new workers – without the expense and trouble of placing an ad or paying a staffing agency.

5. Help reduce the cost of crime for your community. The true cost of crime exceeds millions of dollars in every county America each year, a cost that is decreased when felons return to the work place: "People who break the law need to be held accountable and pay their debt to society. At the same time, the collateral costs of locking up 2.3 million people are piling higher and higher," said Adam Gelb, director of the Pew Center on the States Public Safety Performance Project. According the VERA institute of Justice, the U.S. spends nearly $40 billion a year to house inmates.

6. I can't seem to find good help. That's because you haven't tried hiring felons. Considering them will enlarge the labor pool you can draw from. A 2008 study by the Urban Institute Justice Policy Center found that fewer than 45 percent of felons were employed eight months after being released. That means more than three and half million workers are available. "There are costs associated but the benefits far outweigh the costs. You get a loyal employee, a motivated employee," Hannigan says.

7. Reduce crime & recidivism rate in your community. Many ex-felons return to crime & jail (a.k.a. recidivism) because they can't find a job. Nationally 89% of those ex-felons arrested for returning to crime are unemployed. Please consider that employers who don't hire felons may be contributing to higher crime & recidivism.

8. Join the Crowd? Break the stigma associated with a past criminal offense. It is common to think that only "bad" people commit crimes, yet that stigma ignores the facts. NELP estimates that 70 million U.S. adults have arrest or conviction records based on Bureau of Justice statistics compiled. Tougher sentencing laws, especially for drug offenses, have swelled that total. Society can't afford to banish 70 million people from the workplace.

9. Everybody DOES NOT deserve a second chance – but some do. Those who deserve a second chance are the ones that will demonstrate, not just with words but with their actions that they are sorry for their past mistakes and can prove that their past is in the past. Who wouldn't want to help that person?

10. What difference can I make? More than you think. Look at the costs of housing one inmate per year, compared to the economic impact of having one more productive tax-paying citizen spending money in our economy (instead of draining costs from it), and you can see hiring ex-offenders makes a HUGE difference. According to VERA institute the average cost per state inmate is $31,286 per year. But if that one felon gets a job instead of returning to prison, he or she now contributes to the economy by more than $10,000 a year, according to a Baylor University study.

Did you know you could be breaking the law by NOT hiring a felon? The U.S.

Equal Employment Opportunity Commission says that "An employer's use of an individual's criminal history in making employment decisions may … violate the prohibition against employment discrimination under Title VII of the Civil Rights Act of 1964, as amended."

eeoc.gov/laws/guidance/arrest_conviction.cfm

Here's how to help improve Crime, Recidivism, the Costs of Incarceration, and a Lack of Good Workers. Be part of the solution and HIRE A FELON!

© 2015 by RL Pelshaw

APPENDIX H

GREAT INTERVIEWS & GREATJOBS FOR FELONS

Brought to you by **the National Hire Ex Felons Campaign and** illegaltolegal.org

If you remember only one thing about how to have a great job interview and get a great job it is to **BE PREPARED**. That is what these tips are about: to prepare you for success with jobs and in life. Some of these suggestions may feel awkward to you, but as you use them you'll get better, faster and more confident. Using these common sense tips will help make you stand out and can get you hired quickly!

The biggest issue ex-offenders deal with is how to get a job with a criminal record. Did you know that **89** percent of ex-offenders that are arrested again are unemployed? *Having a job or business could keep you from returning to prison.*

Why not lie about the criminal history? The problem with lying about your criminal past is that it's too easy to find things online. Concealing information is setting yourself up to get fired. Besides 1/3 of Americans have a criminal record, and you've paid your debt to society. People WILL HIRE YOU if you can convince them your past is in your past. Earning their trust starts with telling them the truth about your past.

Here are a couple of ways to deal with the question when it comes up on job applications. On the job application try answering the criminal record question by writing "Yes. I am bondable, will discuss in the interview" or you can answer it with "Yes. I am bondable, but I was convicted of …"

Rather than trying to hide your past, be proactive. Make a short summary statement about your past and your current strengths that shares the truth but doesn't go into great detail. In sales we call that an "elevator speech." It's a sales technique designed to give a motivating summary in about the same amount of time as you are on an elevator. Deliver it in a confident, friendly, and truthful manner. You will earn respect for bringing up your felony yourself. Divulge your past but **don't get into personal problems.** Keep it professional.

The second biggest issue many ex-offenders have to deal with is their attitude. Have a positive attitude, even if you have to "fake it 'till you make it." Having a negative attitude or assuming they will not hire you before you go in creates a self-fulfilling prophecy. No one wants to be around a negative person. Display an attitude that gives people a reason to want to work with you--not against you. Keep this good attitude up even when you had a bad day or are getting worn down. Your *attitude* will determine your *altitude*.

Make it your job to get a job. You may have to put in 100 applications or more before you find work. Don't let that scare you. **You've survived prison, so you can survive anything.** The truth is the odds are against you, and there's only way to beat the odds. *Make applying for jobs your job until you get a job.* You'd spend 40 hours a week working for someone else, so work at least that hard for yourself finding work.

Use the resources at the workforce development center. Get help making a resume. Have a phone number or email available so employers can reach you at. Work closely with your counselor or case officer to find out what resources are available. Check job boards, staffing companies and temp agencies. Ask friends and family if they know of any good jobs. Prepare for job applications like you would for interviews because you never know when a company might save you a return trip and give you an interview on the spot after applying.

Getting a job is a just a numbers game – keep

putting in applications and eventually something will stick. Following these tips will make your efforts more effective, increase your odds, and may reduce the number of applications and interviews you will need to do to be hired.

> ## If you survived prison, you can survive, and do, anything!

MORE TIPS TO HELP YOU NAIL GREAT JOB INTERVIEWS AND GREAT JOBS:

- **LOOK AT THE COMPANY'S WEBSITE BEFORE YOUR APPLICATION OR INTERVIEW** to learn about the company and the details of the position they are hiring for. Make notes of several things on each that you can bring up in your interview. It will impress your interviewer with your professionalism, organization and ability to prepare.

- **HAVE A LIST OF YOUR WORK HISTORY/CREATE A RESUME** before you apply or go on a job interview, which includes dates employed, company contact information, duties, pay and personal references. Every company will ask for the same information, so if you have it in one spot you can complete job applications quicker and with less stress.

- **YOU NEED TO BE YOURSELF.** Be friendly, sincere and believable but not overbearing. Everyone can spot a phony a mile away, and employers generally avoid phonies!

- **YOU DON'T HAVE TO DRESS FANCY, BUT** definitely be clean and wear clothing appropriate for the company and the job you are applying for. If you have tattoos, wear clothes that cover them if possible. Don't overdo cologne, perfume or jewelry either. First impressions will make or break you.

- **YOU'D BE SURPRISED BY WHY YOU SHOULDN'T SMOKE BEFORE THE INTERVIEW.** It's not just so you don't smell smoky. *Employers have wised up to smokers* and have noticed that smokers take more work breaks than non-smokers take. Smokers also often have more health issues than non-smoking workers. All things being equal the company **will hire** the non-smoker over the smoker. Improve your odds and don't walk in smelling like an ashtray, which is exactly how you smell when you smoke in your car on the way to the interview. No, you can't "air out" or cover it up; that never works.

- **TRY TO BRING A DECENT FOLDER WITH A NOTEPAD** that you can use to keep your resumes and work history notes, references, etc.

- **BEING EARLY ISN'T JUST ABOUT PUNCTUALITY.** Getting there 10 minutes early is a great way to relax and prepare for your interview, and you're sending a good message to your potential new employer. Check in with the company when you first get there. Often they'll have you complete application paperwork. Remember to be nice to the receptionist, and act professionally while you wait. Some interviewers will ask the receptionist about you later. While you're waiting, get a drink of water and make sure you don't have a scratchy throat. Make sure your breath smells good. If you chew gum or a mint, make sure you get rid of it before you meet your appointment. Take the time and use the restroom. Tuck your shirt in. Relax. Get your head in the game. Breathe.

- **DON'T BE TOO EARLY.** Showing up more than 15-20 minutes early is as bad as being late. Yes, you're eager, but being too eager can inconvenience the person you'll be meeting. It's better to wait outside than show up too early.

- **TURN OFF YOUR CELL PHONE OR THE RINGER** once you're at the company. Don't respond to any texts during your interview. That's the fastest way to the circular file. Respect them enough and show enough interest in the job to turn it off or leave it in your car during your interview.

- **WHEN YOU MEET SOMEONE** in the company, give them a good firm handshake, try to maintain good eye contact and always ask for a business card if they don't offer you one. Having their card makes the task of following up much easier for you. It also shows them that you are interested enough to ask for one. Sincerely thank them for their time, and be pleasant, professional, and genuine.

- **HERE'S THE BEST TIP**: Within the first couple of minutes after the introductions, repeat his or her name back a few times until you remember it. For instance, if asked about your previous work history, you can say, "Thanks for asking Mrs. Jones, my work history is...."

- **EARLY IN THE INTERVIEW** try to ask "what exactly does the job entail? And please describe what a person has to do to succeed in that job." During the rest of the interview try to steer your answers to key points the interviewer is interested in.

- **IF YOU'RE NERVOUS, JUST SLOW DOWN**, breathe deeply and think about what you are going to say. You can even tell the person you're a little nervous and that getting this job is important to you. They will appreciate your directness and honesty. Usually such honesty will not only make you feel more at ease but the interviewer will sympathize. He or she might even remember you in a good way.

- **ANSWER QUESTIONS AS DIRECTLY AS POSSIBLE,** but less is more when answering questions. Be honest, but the interviewer doesn't need to hear every detail. Going into too much detail could kill their interest in you if they think you talk too much. Try to think of how you would react if you were doing the interviewing. Ask yourself "what would you want to know about you?"

- **BE CONSIDERATE AND NEVER INTERRUPT THEM.** Show respect and appreciation.

- **TAKE NOTES WHEN THEY ARE TALKING** or answering your questions. This shows you're organized, engaged and willing to put forth extra effort.

- **SILENCE IS OK** – there doesn't have to be constant conversation during the whole time together. Use any silence to think about the interview and how the interviewer is responding to you.

- **WATCH FOR BODY LANGUAGE** and act or react accordingly. Are they engaged and leaning forward, or have they lost interest and are slouching? Are they writing down your answers?

- **PROJECT THE RIGHT BODY LANGUAGE** and be engaged, leaning forward with eye contact. Don't slouch. Be the confident professional that they need to hire instead of the bum wasting their time. If you're good at this, you can mimic positive body language signals the interviewer offers, like a nodding head or a smile. That is a powerful subconscious way to get people to start accepting and considering you.

- **HAVE QUESTIONS READY** to ask them when they are done. If they don't mention it, politely ask if you can ask a few questions. Before you start with your questions you can say, "I had a list of questions prepared. Please give me a moment to see how many of them you've already answered." If you don't have any more questions just say "Mr. Jones you've done a great job of answering all the questions I had."

- **MAKE SURE YOU ASK THEM** what the next step is or when you can follow up with them about the job. Some interviewers automatically don't consider anyone that isn't interested enough in the job to find out what they have to do next.

- Here's some **"OLD SCHOOL" ADVICE** that will REALLY set you apart from the rest. Go to the dollar store and buy a cheap packet of "thank-you" notes. A day or two later mail them a short, thoughtful, handwritten note thanking them for the interview and asking them to keep you in consideration. If you can't send them a thank-you note, at least send them an email or phone call thanking them for the consideration.

- **PRACTICE** these skills by grabbing a friend and role-playing the interview process. Repeat until you feel prepared.

- **EVALUATE** how you did. Every job interview gives the opportunity to practice being a better job candidate. Look back at what you did well, what you did poorly, and what you could have done to perform better in the interview. Doing so will make the next interviews smoother and more effective for you.

We want to hear how you did with interviewing and how these tips helped. If you have any suggestions or tips we can pass on to others please contact us. Share with us on our Facebook Page, Twitter account, or by emailing us at info@hireexfelons.org.

For those ex-felons who still can't find a job that pays enough to keep away from returning to crime we have resources to show them how to use their life skills to start their own business, and hopefully become an employer themselves.

Buy a copy of **Illegal to Legal: Business Success for (Ex) Criminals** for an offender, ex-offender, or person at risk to offend, or their families. Check www.illegaltolegal.org for many free resources as well.

Please "like us" on Facebook and follow us on Twitter.

To reorder this brochure please contact
www.hireexfelons.org
info@illegaltolegal.org
© 2015 by The Pelshaw Group

APPENDIX I

YOUR CRIMINAL HISTORY AND JOB INTERVIEWS

from Pelshaw's Blog
illegaltolegal.org © 2015

At the time I am writing this blog, President Obama has just announced an executive order that "bans the box" on most federal job applications. "Banning the Box" doesn't yet mean an employer can't ask about your criminal history. If you want to succeed in your job search, you need to be prepared to properly address your criminal history on job applications, and in interviews.

Given that so many employers discriminate against someone with a criminal history, I've been asked if you should simply lie about the criminal history on the job application. Perhaps, but if (or when) your employer finds out, they will fire you for lying on the job application. Lying is not the way to build trust. I recommend if you are within a year after being released, that you answer the criminal history question by saying "yes, but bondable." The employer will always ask what that means. They will automatically assume that if you are bondable then your criminal offense must not be that bad.

The federal government provides free fidelity bonds for employers hiring felons out of prison a year or less. These bonds are easily available at bonds4jobs.com and provide a form of free insurance to employers.

Now you have their attention. Here is how to use it to your advantage:

Have you ever heard of an "elevator pitch?" That is a short sales pitch designed to explain the benefits and strengths of a product, given in about the time it takes to ride and elevator. Felons applying for jobs need to have two elevator pitches practiced and ready to use on a new employer.

Certainly you've seen it on TV where a doctor tells someone bad news. They aren't emotional, but they plainly and directly say the bad news without explanation, detail, or apology. They do follow up the bad news with a solution or a course of action that is short and direct. Your first "elevator pitch" should mention your charge, the fact that you've served time, and that you have taken responsibility and put your past in the past. If you're on probation, let the employer know that is to their advantage since they will have an outside party with a vested interest in making sure you are the best worker they ever had.

Most people believe in second chances. You need to convince them that even though everybody isn't ready for a chance, you are. Have specific examples of how you changed and what you learned inside your first elevator pitch.

Assume you were just asked "do you have any criminal history." Here is an example of an elevator pitch designed to deal with criminal history:

> Yes, unfortunately, I, like 100 million other Americans, do have a criminal history. The fact that nearly 30% of us have one shows that we all have a past, right? I assure you my past is in the past. I made mistakes, but I took responsibilities for them, and paid for them. This is how I put my past in the past: (insert short, personal accomplishments, changes, etc.)

The second elevator pitch should include the things that make you an outstanding worker, and why the employer should hire you.

Also, mention the federal work opportunity tax credit that is easily available if they hire you. Many employers have achieved great bottom line success, and enjoyed committed and loyal workers, by hiring ex-felons. It's your job to simply inform them of this in a way that makes them want to hire you.

Here is an example of an elevator pitch designed to highlight your benefits as a worker, if you have relevant work experience:

> I understand you are looking to hire a person with the following skills (insert skills the employer said they wanted for the job, and then briefly tell them how you have them).

Here is an example of an elevator pitch designed to highlight your benefits as a worker, if they know about your criminal history, or if you don't have much work experience:

> Yes, I may not be the most experienced applicant you are considering, but I promise you, I'm the most dedicated applicant. Not having much experience means I'm a clean slate that doesn't carry the baggage of bad work habits you need to retrain. That doesn't make me a risk; it makes me an asset. I will be the hardest worker you've ever seen, and I learn fast. I'll be on time, with a great attitude, and never complain about things. I will appreciate the chance you've given me to prove my benefits to you. You will have gained my loyalty, respect, and gratitude. When is the last time you hired someone who truly appreciated the chance to work? I'm that person! I come with a tax credit to help subsidize my wages, and a fidelity bond to eliminate any risk or concern you may have for hiring me. So what do you say? Are you willing to give me a chance?

Of course, these are examples of elevator pitches. You will want to put them in your own words, tailored for your own circumstances. Practice them until they sound natural, and not rehearsed. After each time you use it, critique it and adjust as necessary. Good luck!

According to a statement from the Equal Employment Opportunity Commission, it may be illegal for employers to discriminate against someone because of their criminal history. The U.S. Equal Employment Opportunity Commission says that "An employer's use of an individual's criminal history in making employment decisions may ... violate the prohibition against employment discrimination under Title VII of the Civil Rights Act of 1964, as amended."(see: eeoc.gov/laws/guidance/arrest_conviction.cfm).

Be careful how you use that information in a job interview. Most employers detest being threatened with an employment discrimination lawsuit. Even if, or when, they discriminate against you, it is likely an employer can find an excuse to cover the fact they are discriminating against you.

I think selling yourself as the best job candidate, and winning them over on the bottom-line benefits of hiring you, is the best way to get hired. If you feel that you might be discriminated against, perhaps in the interview, when you are disclosing your criminal history, you can also say:

> I'm glad you are a law-biding employer that wouldn't discriminate against a job applicant because of their criminal history.

If they ask about that simply tell them what the Equal Employment Opportunity Commission says above. Be informative and helpful, not threatening or accusatory.

Getting a good job is about selling yourself. Any good salesman knows it takes a lot of "no's" before you get a "yes." Don't give up, keep trying, keep practicing, and keep improving your interview skills with every job interview you have. Eventually you will get the job you want. Otherwise, you can always apply what you've learned from this book and start a business!

BIBLIOGRAPHY

CHAPTER 1

A published study titled: "Growth in the U.S. Ex - Felon and Ex - Prisoner Population, 1948 to 2010" by Shannon, Uggen, Thompson, Schnittler and Massoglia, © 2010.

Cable News Network, News Report, December 10, 2013.

Rev. T.D. Jakes, paraphrased quote made while preaching.

Corbett, Michael F., *The Outsourcing Revolution*, Dearborn © 2004.

A published study titled: "Recidivism of Prisoners Released in 30 States in 2005: Patterns from 2005 to 2010" Alexia D. Cooper, Ph.D., Matthew R. Durose, Howard N. Synder, Ph.D. © 2014.

U.S. Equal Employment Opportunity Commission. [Internet] 2014. Available from: http://www.eeoc.gov/laws/guidance/arrest_conviction.cfm

Ecclesiastes 11:4, *New King James Version of the Bible*, Thomas Nelson, © 1982.

CHAPTER 2

Mark Twain Quote. [Internet] 2014. The Goodreads.com website. Available from: http://www.goodreads.com/quotes/585578-the-secret-of-success-is-making-your-vocation-your-vacation

Space Shuttle facts. [Internet] 2014. The Caltech.edu website. Available from: http://coolcosmos.ipac.caltech.edu/ask/268-How-much-did-the-Space-Shuttle-weigh-

Hassig, Ross. *Mexico and the Spanish Conquest*. Longman Group UK Limited, © 1994.

CHAPTER 3

Dave Ramsey quote from his DVD series "Financial Peace University," © 2009

Zig Ziglar quote. [Internet] 2014. From the Official Zig Ziglar Quote Library at www.Zigziglar.com/quotes.

"Mary Kay Ash," *Entreprenuer Magazine*, October 10, 2008 (writer not cited in article)

Zig Ziglar quote. [Internet] 2014. From the Official Zig Ziglar Quote Library at www.Zigziglar.com/quotes.

CHAPTER 4
Small Business Administration Frequently Asked Questions. [Internet] 2014. From the Small Business Administration website www.sba.gov. Available at: http://www.sba.gov/sites/default/files/advocacy/FAQ_March_2014_0.pdf

CHAPTER 5

Zig Ziglar quote. [Internet] 2014. From the Official Zig Ziglar Quote Library at www.Zigziglar.com/quotes.

Wooden, John and Jamison, Steve, *Wooden on Leadership*, McGraw-Hill, © 2005.

Tony Robbins quote. [Internet] 2014. From the Brainyquote.com website.

John Maxwell quote extracted from his teaching lessons, The Maximum Impact Club, John Maxwell Company, www.johnmaxwell.com

Small Business Administration Frequently Asked Questions. [Internet] 2014. From the Small Business Administration website www.sba.gov. Available at: http://www.sba.gov/sites/default/files/advocacy/FAQ_March_2014_0.pdf

CHAPTER 6

John Maxwell quote extracted from his teaching lessons, The Maximum Impact Club, John Maxwell Company, www.johnmaxwell.com

Godin, Seth. *Purple Cow: Transform Your Business by Being Remarkable*, Portfolio, © 2003.

Heffernan, Tim. "All Politics Is Still Local " article in Esquire Magazine, September 29, 2010.

Luke 6:31, paraphrased from the *New King James Version of the Bible*, Thomas Nelson, © 1982.

[Internet] 2014, from the website bonds4jobs.com

Roman, Kenneth, "The House That Ogilvy Built," Strategy and Business, February 29, 2009, Spring 2009, Issue 54.

John Wesley quote, Million Leaders Mandate Volume I Notebook 6, page 6, Equip Foundation, © 2003.

Kiyosaki, Robert and Lechter, Sharon L., *Rich Dad Poor Dad,* Grand Central Publishing, © 2001.

Joyce Meyers quote. [Internet] 2014. From the Brainyquote.com website: brainyquote.com

---

NOTE ON SOURCES OF ALL SUCCESS SNAPSHOTS:

Nearly all Success Snapshots were based on individual interviews or personal life experience by the author, and except as noted within individual Success Snapshots the sources of each have opted to remain confidential. The author has maintained the source materials for the interviews. Additional sources used in the Success Snapshots are noted as follows:

SUCCESS SNAPSHOT: TRUCKING

John Maxwell quote extracted from his teaching lessons, The Maximum Impact Club, John Maxwell Company, johnmaxwell.com

SUCCESS SNAPSHOT: JANITORIAL SERVICES

John Maxwell quote extracted from his teaching lessons, The Maximum Impact Club, John Maxwell Company, johnmaxwell.com

SUCCESS SNAPSHOT: WAREHOUSE GYM/HEALTH CLUB

IHRSA Trend Report, Updated 6/17/2013, International Health, Racquet and Sportsclub Association's (IHRSA), [Internet] 2014, Available at: http://www.ihrsa.org/media-center/2013/5/8/585-million-americans-utilize-health-clubs.html

Kiyosaki, Robert and Lechter, Sharon L., *Rich Dad Poor Dad,* Grand Central Publishing, © 2001.

Success Snapshot: Personal Security Services
Maxwell, John, *The 21 Irrefutable Laws of Leadership: Follow Them and People will Follow You*, Thomas Nelson Publishers, © 2007.

Success Snapshot: Detailing Business
Seitz, Rick, "Detailing 101" article in GM High Tech Performance Magazine, March 2014, p 69-74.

US Census Bureau, [Internet] 2014. A report from January 2014 accessed from census.gov

Seitz, Rick, *ibid.*

Success Snapshot: Rental Business
Buffet, Mary and Clark, David, *Buffetology*, Fireside, © 1997.

Success Snapshot: Mobile Homes
US Census Bureau, [Internet] 2014. A report from January 2014 accessed from census.gov

Success Snapshot: The Pusher
"Big O" personal interview at Leavenworth Federal Prison Camp, December 15, 2013

Zig Ziglar quote. [Internet] 2014. From the Official Zig Ziglar Quote Library at Zigziglar.com/quotes

INDEX

TRUTH ABOUT PRISON · NETWORK

TRUTH ABOUT PRISON NETWORK

We at the TRUTH ABOUT PRISON NETWORK (TAP-X) strive to be the "go-to company" serving inmates and their families providing a wide range of services.

We help inmates and their families through the entire journey of incarceration; from the first day in until the last day out.

We strive to be the most comprehensive and complete free source of information about the federal and state prison systems in the United States for inmates and the loved ones that also serve time with them.

We offer unique services like:

THE TAP-X PHOTO APP: Pictures from home are some of the most treasured possessions in prison. Send photos as easy as texting a picture through the free TAP-X Photo App, even internationally! Once submitted, we use professional photo printing equipment and process all orders within one business day.

THE TAP-X STORE where inmates can purchase needed items including books, magazines, e-cards and more. Send us an email at info@tap-x.com for more information and to fund your account.

FREE NEWSLETTER SIGN-UP: Inmates: simply add INFO@TAP-X.COM to your contact list and receive: Prison News, Helpful Information, Quotes, Riddles, Fantasy Football, Giveaways and more...

Everyone else please visit the website **www.truthaboutprison.com** to subscribe.

THE TAP-X WEBSITE HAS:

- **Information:** On family support groups, references for loved ones, as well as links and contact information for every prison, whether federal or state, in the United States.

- **Prison Questionnaires:** We give questionnaires to currently incarcerated inmates in various prisons and we publish their full answers on our website.

- **Forums:** TAP-X has over 1,500 forums, one for each Federal and State Prison in the United States, providing information about what happens at specific prisons.

- **Personal Services:** Confidentially email questions and/or have a conference call with former inmates/guards to get all of your questions answered.

- **Helpful Links:** to other resources.

Help us spread the word about TAP-X by visiting our website, liking us on Facebook, and following us on Twitter. Thanks again for your continued support!

SUBSCRIBE TODAY, AND SHARE
OUR SERVICES WITH A FRIEND
OR LOVED ONE!

R.L. Pelshaw
Speaker, Author, Entrepreneur

Need an entertaining, inspiring, challenging, educational speaker?

R.L. Pelshaw is available for:

- Keynote address.
- Events (speaker forum, fireside chat, panelist, breakout session).
- Workshops (professional development, corporate retreats, training, seminars).
- Fundraisers (nonprofits, schools, churches, community organizations, etc.).

Pelshaw is a seasoned global communicator with expertise in these areas:

- Leadership development
- Starting over in life
- Achieving something from nothing
- Entrepreneurship and business growth
- Reentry after prison
- Surviving prison
- Poverty to self-employment
- Growing up in a multi-racial household
- Real Estate development
- Economic Incentives
- Fund raising

To book Pelshaw:

Email: bob@pelshawgroup.com
Call: 402-932-7777

Online inquiry:
www.illegaltolegal.org/public_speaking

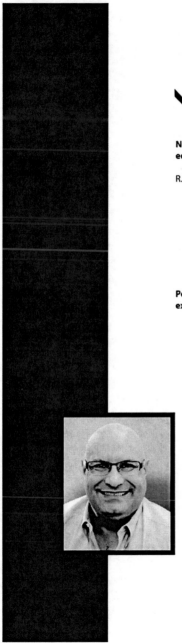

257